P9-DVC-996

M

THE LIMITS OF METAPHOR

A Study of Melville, Conrad, and Faulkner

THE LIMITS OF
METAPHOR

A Study of Melville, Conrad, and Faulkner

By JAMES GUETTI

CORNELL UNIVERSITY PRESS

Ithaca and London

Copyright © 1967 by Cornell University

CORNELL UNIVERSITY PRESS

First published 1967
Second printing 1969

Standard Book Number 8014-0166-6

Library of Congress Catalog Card Number 67-10489

PRINTED IN THE UNITED STATES OF AMERICA
BY VALLEY OFFSET, INC.
BOUND BY VAIL-BALLOU PRESS, INC.

Acknowledgments

FOR permission to reprint quotations I would like to thank the following publishers: John Grant Booksellers, Ltd., for *The Works of Joseph Conrad;* Houghton Mifflin Company for Herman Melville's *Moby-Dick,* edited by Alfred Kazin; Random House, Inc., for William Faulkner's *Absalom, Absalom!,* copyright 1936 by William Faulkner and renewed 1964 by Estelle Faulkner and Jill Faulkner Summers.

Chapter III, " 'Heart of Darkness': The Failure of Imagination," first appeared, in different form, in *The Sewanee Review,* LXXIII (July–September, 1965), copyright by The University of the South.

J. G.

New Brunswick, New Jersey
May 1966

Contents

I. Introduction 1

II. The Languages of *Moby-Dick* 12

III. "Heart of Darkness": The Failure of
　　Imagination 46

IV. *Absalom, Absalom!*: The Extended Simile. . 69

V. Ramifications 109

VI. The Range of the Problem 132

VII. Conclusion: The Instability of Metaphor . . 154

List of Works Cited 190

Index 193

THE LIMITS OF METAPHOR

A Study of Melville, Conrad, and Faulkner

CHAPTER I

Introduction

THERE is little question that the English and American novel—especially in the past half-century or so—has inclined toward new forms and narrative techniques. But the causes of this tendency, as I see it, are more radical than is suggested by describing them in terms that are social ("modern life is complicated, and hence the novel...") or religious ("God has disappeared, and thus the novel...") or narrowly technical ("the sequential narrative is no longer useful"). By concentrating upon a few important works of prose fiction, I shall attempt to show that the development of a major tradition in the novel reveals more and more clearly a fundamental imaginative instability, reveals a failure to compose experience in any way or to create coherent metaphorical structures of any sort. And while I would not presume to declare that social or religious or technical considerations are irrelevant to this formal disintegration in the novel, I would suggest that the actual verbal phenomena of the disintegration are more important. It is likely, I think, that what are often seen as forces behind literary change are in fact simply parallel developments from other contexts. The roots of such change might better be looked for in a lower and more common denominator: in the fundamental imaginative process of creating, discarding, and re-creating order and, more specifically, in the verbal difficulties that arise as this process—from causes largely within itself—accelerates. These difficulties, as I shall suggest later, appear to be implicit in the very nature of language and become obvious as the imagination is called upon more and more frequently to create, by manipulating the diversities of its perceptions, new and stable order.

I shall try to define this problem of imagination by discussing in detail single works—although I shall later deal with each author more widely—by Melville, Conrad, and Faulkner; these writers, I think, are the novelists most intensely and explicitly concerned with the inadequacy of language, and the essentials of their concern will be best illuminated by a close examination of *Moby-Dick,* "Heart of Darkness," and *Absalom, Absalom!* My basic interest is the particular sort of rhetoric exhibited in these works, the characteristic manner in which narrators such as Ishmael, Marlow, and Quentin Compson approach a problematic experience by surrounding it with disparate allusions and suggestions, never emphasizing a single perspective as definitive, and constantly relying, at crucial moments, upon the nearly simultaneous use of separate kinds of language—separate vocabularies—and upon similes of the greatest but vaguest dimensions. By this central method, these novelists create a sense of disparity between language in general and something that appears to be inexpressible, which we might call "life" or "truth" or "reality." Above all, however, this "reality" is defined as something beyond the powers of imagination, and in the

2

Introduction

pages that follow I have termed it, for this reason, the "ineffable."

Immediately we are dealing with a paradox, and it is the first, probably, of many: if a reader becomes aware of some "ineffable reality," then language, it would seem, has not failed. It is the terms of the communication effected, however, that are most important, for the suggestion of an ineffable reality depends upon a recognition of the insufficiency of language and is communicated largely by means of this insufficiency. As this idea of the ineffable develops through Melville, Conrad, and Faulkner, furthermore, a reader's attention is drawn more and more to the fact that his awareness of an inexpressible "reality" depends upon the admitted instability of all imaginative attempts to apprehend it. Within the books that I have mentioned, the idea of the ineffable is shown to be dissolving: the emphasis shifts in "Heart of Darkness" from the idea of a "reality" beyond language to the limitations within language that were seen as evidence for the existence of such a reality. The idea of an "ineffable" for Conrad becomes more insistently a matter of failure. The manner in which Melville suggests—by means of focusing upon the limitations of words—the reality of something beyond words becomes for Conrad more nearly a flat inability to penetrate through or beyond language by means of language or an inability to demonstrate by means of the insufficiencies within language the existence of something outside it. The "ineffable," in this way, approaches the "nothingness."

In *Absalom, Absalom!* Faulkner pursues the problem even further: the idea of an ineffable reality is never explicitly recognized, and the complexities and confusion of the narrative indicate only an incapacity to compose language itself. The matter is no longer defined in terms of a tension between language and a nonlinguistic reality but in terms of insoluble tensions within language. The characteristic narrative structure of the hunt or the search that we encounter in *Moby-Dick* and "Heart of Darkness" becomes in Faulkner a search for the right words, a matter of telling and retelling, and the narrative difficulty is that of using language in such a way as to prevent one's recognition of the arbitrariness and exclusiveness of composed linguistic systems. The kind of linguistic complexity that was employed in *Moby-Dick* to suggest the ineffable often becomes in Faulkner's work, for reasons that I shall discuss at length, simply a confusion.

It should be clear that, speaking generally, the novel with which I am concerned here is not the novel that exposes the failure of social communication or civilized morality within a civilized context. The focus there is sharper, the vision narrower: the insufficiency displayed is not that of language in general but that of certain vocabularies among and opposed to other vocabularies. The sort of novel that I shall consider, however, is one that thrives—at least at the beginning of the tradition, while the illusion of a reality beyond language persists— upon literal and figurative distance from an ordered world of any sort. In this respect, it should be apparent that an emphasis upon the problematic qualities of language creates a kind of prose fiction quite different from that illuminated by criticism that is predominantly social or moral—or by the sorts of criticism most prevalent in England and America.

I would suggest, in fact, that a general approach to the novel like that of F. R. Leavis, as useful as it has proved, not only leaves entire—and important—areas of fiction undescribed but also may construct unnecessary barriers to the sort of inquiry that I shall attempt. We may consider, for example, the famous passage from Leavis' discussion of "Heart of Darkness":

Conrad must here stand convicted of borrowing the arts of the magazine-writer (who has borrowed his, shall we say, from Kipling and Poe) in order to impose upon his readers and on himself, for thrilled response, a "significance" that is merely an emotional insistence on the presence of what he can't produce. The insistence betrays the absence, the willed "intensity" the nullity. He is intent on making a virtue out of not knowing what he means.[1]

It is important to recognize the possibility, on the contrary, that Conrad may know very well what he means and know too that what he means is not enough: he may be dramatizing the very inability that Leavis describes as a weakness of the prose, and it is important, also, to realize that by examining the text with this in mind we might discover ample reasons for such a dramatization. We may note also the kind of assumption made in Leavis' criticism—and in most criticism that accepts his tenets—by which a largely undramatic and narrative uncertainty automatically becomes bad writing. The explanation of this assumption—which, to one who reads Conrad in conjunction with Melville and Faulkner, or perhaps in conjunction simply with novelists of the twentieth century, is simply a mistake—may lie in the strength of Leavis' faith in language and in his conviction that reality is expressed in "social"—in the novel, "dramatic"—interaction. He appears to feel that because there is no indubitable reality that is not socially or dramatically definable, we may forget about

[1]*The Great Tradition* (Garden City: Doubleday & Co., 1954), p. 219.

the problem, and it may be that he preserves his belief in language exactly by deeming of secondary interest those works of literature that would question it.

I would not object to this approach so strenuously—for, again, its importance is clear—if I did not think that such a "faith in language" entails a satisfaction with limitations of language that are merely assumed. By insisting upon certain linguistic capacities and realities, in other words, critics like Leavis often sell language short. As I shall try to show, the novelist's self-conscious and sustained exploration of the capacities of language in an extended narrative may constitute the most suggestive and powerful use of language possible.

The attitude that I have associated, perhaps too insistently, with Leavis, however, is important in the context of my discussion, for it brings to our attention a difficult issue in the analysis to follow. One is constantly forced to consider and to determine the point at which an expression of failure or near-failure becomes a failure of expression. As I have suggested earlier, the difficulty of imagining order has frequently become the subject of the novel, the problem of a given narrative. Yet this matter is so genuinely problematic that it may encroach upon the order of the narrative itself; by presenting the idea of a fundamental incoherence in experience, the novel itself may become incoherent.

A novelist cannot seriously posit a fundamental disorder in experience if the neatness of his technique belies this supposed disorder at every turn; there is no way, in other words, to express the problem of imaginative order if it is not a real problem in the narrative, and if it is a real problem then it inevitably has important effects upon the form of the narrative. And yet an incoherent narrative, even if juxtaposed with the assertion of an inability to compose experience, cannot stand for the expression of the failure: an incoherent narrative, of course, expresses nothing, not even incoherence. Thus we are liable to find, in a novel that does express crucial imaginative difficulties, a complicated sort of rhetorical balance, and at the most difficult moments of this inquiry, as I shall try to show, failure and success may be nearly indistinguishable.

But there is another apparent contradiction in this matter—one that is related to those already mentioned—that I should at least outline at this point. It may seem curious, at various moments in the following pages, that my assertion of a basic disintegration in a novel is so often nearly simultaneous with my praise of the language of that same novel. Aside from a general plea that the reader sustain his patience until my arguments are complete, I can give two reasons for what would seem critical double vision. First, although the rhetorical mode I have sketched is perhaps the most successful method of fiction, although it may suggest a world beyond language, greater than language, this rhetoric does so because it fails, given our usual assumptions about language, to accomplish what it ought. It fails to structure, fails to control, and it fails, finally, if communication can be said to depend upon defined verbal sense, to communicate. It may be that the "failure" here is due to our own attitude toward language, an attitude that, if it is not simply a mistake, is at least totally ambivalent. Our expectation of consistent and literal verbal sense is perfectly adequate to measure, for instance, the success of more commonplace communication, but this same expectation and assumption of the value of consistent "sense" proves insufficient for the uses of language that, in literature and life, we find most interesting and most effective. This is not to say, of course, that the problem of sense and, more significantly, order is not a serious problem, for the novelists I have mentioned themselves invoke this question of ultimate coherence: they demand that we consider their work, at least in part, as the dramatized attempt to achieve some final imaginative stability. But to say that the attempt fails is not necessarily to say that these writers fail as novelists. More generally and more important, the failure of language to structure experience in an ultimate way does not necessarily equal the failure of language; this failure may reveal, as I think it does in the novelists with whom I am concerned here, the most important kind of success.

The second reason for my asserting so often that language and imagination in these writers are genuinely problematic is a simpler matter. The methods of these novelists, no matter how effective and successful at any given moment, rely upon the kind of rhetorical failure that I have sketched above. Their methods are therefore fundamentally unstable and inevitably end, if extended, in imaginative collapse. For even if we can say that the structural, ordering function is not the only function of language, we must recognize, I think, that language and imagination depend upon this function or at least upon the possibility, the expectation, of it, and the consistent denial of the possibility of order prepares for the general disintegration of imaginative capacity. That is to say that while imaginative disorder need not, in any given work or instance of language, imply unambiguous imaginative failure, the continual preoccupation with such disorder does result, finally, in the collapse even of the rhetorical mode most closely associated with this preoccupation. As the problem develops—both in the work of a single novelist and through the work of many novelists—the incoherency presented necessarily impinges, for reasons that I shall discuss later, more and more upon the presentation itself. My discussion of this rhetoric of failure in Melville, Conrad, and Faulkner can only be regarded as an introduction. Although I shall attempt to define the problem by concentrating upon writers and works that are for me the most striking examples of it, the tradition of prose fiction, and of literature, that is involved has a much greater range and consequence than has been heretofore understood, and the extent of the tradition implies a recognition among writers of certain qualities of language that, however fundamental, is not as prevalent among critics as one would like. I can only hope that my investigations will provoke more general and more flexible studies.

The range of my treatment, then, will be narrow. I shall seldom make connections between my conclusions about the three novelists I have mentioned, for instance, and other novels or other literature, even when such connections seem obvious. But I hope that my treatment is narrow because it is intensive. My intention is to break down this problem of imagination, in the three important instances of it that I shall describe at length, into its simplest possible terms, to describe the verbal phenomena associated with this question as completely as I can. And thus since my present alternatives are to mention other writers either briefly or not at all, I have usually chosen not at all unless I have been reasonably sure that other, short examples will clarify, rather than obscure, the questions at hand.

My method throughout is close textual—that is to say, verbal—analysis, for this, as I see it, is the most conclusive of the methods of literary criticism, especially when one is examining, in a light that is relatively new, works that have been written about and over many times before with largely dissimilar results. Regarding my treatment of the contributions of other critics and scholars of these writers and of the novel at large, I shall mention such contributions only if they are relevant to my purpose. I shall generally refrain from any further mention of critics to disagree with them, since I prefer to devote myself to the internal demands of my own argument and since those to whom such disagreements matter or who know extant criticism well enough to understand fully the importance of any given disagreement will recognize the points of divergence without my aid.

I may simply note at this point that recent criticism has recognized that the various thematic conflicts expressed in *Moby-Dick,* "Heart of Darkness," and *Absalom, Absalom!* are remarkably tenacious. But this criticism has usually either emphasized the ingenious and complicated manner in which such conflicts seem finally to be resolved or accomplished its own "resolution" by showing that these conflicts are part of a stock set of attitudes from literary tradition or intellectual history. At the last a fundamental, unified "theme" is elucidated, whose familiarity often belies the seriousness and intensity of the conflicts from which it arose.

Such attempts, as I see it, have done little but emphasize their arbitrariness, and my own purpose, therefore, is twofold. First, I shall describe the linguistic techniques that have given rise to the thematic conflicts I have mentioned. In this way I shall try to demonstrate a more consistent narrative concern in these novels than the frequent labeling and relabeling of such conflicts in the terms of various literary and intellectual traditions have indicated. Second, I shall question completely this matter of ultimate resolution—which critics so often suppose must be there—in order to show that the basic emphasis in Melville, Conrad, and Faulkner is not upon some ultimate idea of truth or reality, or even upon some standard ideological dichotomy or paradox, but upon the unreality of imaginative structure of any sort and upon the radical linguistic nature—as opposed to the ideological nature— of the problem of order.

CHAPTER II

The Languages of Moby-Dick

BEFORE the narrative of *Moby-Dick* begins, Melville presents a reader with "whale" in thirteen languages, and subsequently with a group of extracts containing allusions to the whale from the Bible, from poetry, from histories of whaling, from whaling songs, and so on. A reader is therefore, at the outset, asked to detour; if we are to know the whale, it seems from these opening pages that our imaginative progress must be indirect if not circuitous. The narrative itself corroborates this expectation. The explicit presentation of the most important elements of the story as various kinds of language is characteristic of *Moby-Dick* and furthermore may be seen to become the narrative concern of Ishmael and the dramatic problem of Ahab.

The narrative of the book takes three basic forms: In the first place, Melville often makes use of sustained, special vocabularies in describing whales and whaling, and although we have little difficulty in making sense of these vocabularies in terms of their internal, word-to-word consistency, when we attempt to apply them to more essential matters—Moby Dick, for example—they seem remote, arbitrary, and artificial. Secondly, although the narrator employs many separate vocabularies that seem to originate in himself, he also presents a reader with many more in the form of allusions to and reports of what someone else has said or might say about whales and Moby Dick. Thus we may be given, almost simultaneously, a firsthand, dramatic account of a fight with a sperm whale, an allusion to a Greek myth which might be relevant, an account of what the most superstitious character in Nantucket has said about similar fights, and a reference to the fabulous remarks of some historians of whaling. These allusions are part of a large body of figurative language in *Moby-Dick*—language that is ostentatiously qualified by means of either its deliberate presentation as allusion and report or an explicit figurative tag, an "as if" or a "seemed." Such qualifications are frequently belied, however, by the intensity with which the figures themselves are presented; in this manner they create an illusion of distinctness in opposition to the vagueness produced by their multiplicity, the freedom with which they replace one another, and their avowed qualifications. The third narrative method to be found in *Moby-Dick* is the use of figurative language that within itself is both complex and unresolved, language that is significant as an explicit or implicit admission by the narrator that he cannot know or say what is most important.

The first technique is perhaps best exemplified in the chapter entitled "Cetology." Here the whale is treated specifically as a linguistic definition, *"a spouting fish with a horizontal tail."*[1] The emphasis on language becomes

[1]Herman Melville, *Moby-Dick or, The Whale,* ed. Alfred Kazin (Boston: Houghton Mifflin Company, 1956), p. 118. The text is that of the first American edition with minor and reasonable alterations. All subsequent references to *Moby-Dick* are to this edition.

more apparent, more artificial, and more ambiguously jocular when whales are subsequently classified as if they were themselves great bodies of language: "First: According to magnitude I divide the whales into three primary BOOKS (subdivisible into Chapters), and these shall comprehend them all, both small and large" (118). This cataloguing of whales as folios, octavos, and duodecimos may well be a joke, but the book-whale category has serious relevance, in a manner that I shall discuss, to others ways of talking about whales to be found in "Cetology."

"Already," the narrator remarks as "Cetology" begins, "we are boldly launched upon the deep; but soon we shall be lost in its unshored, harborless immensities" (116). And so we must first systematize whales, which is "to grope down into the bottom of the sea after them; to have one's hands among the unspeakable foundations, ribs, and very pelvis of the world" (117). In its suggestion of great depths and unspeakable secrets, this introduction is significant in the negative, for what follows is both shallow and easily said. The various names of the whales are listed, the origin of these names given, the habitat of the "fish" noted, and the physical characteristics of each described as closely and as exactly as knowledge permits. After a few such accounts, however, the narrator throws up his hands and declares that the only system that can possibly succeed is his own "Bibliographical" system, "for it alone is practicable" (121). He nonetheless continues with the same sort of descriptive details as before, concluding with the porpoise, and if a reader wonders whether the inquiry has not strayed from the subject of the great whale, the narrator answers by repeating his definition of "what a whale is—i.e. a spouting fish, with a horizontal tail" (124).

The Languages of Moby-Dick

Even if we decide that the bibliographical system is humorously presented, that it is "practicable" simply because the relation between whale and book is dependent only upon an arbitrary notion of relative size, we cannot ignore the more serious, implied connection between talking about porpoises as if they were whales and talking about whales in general as if they were a group of words, a definition. The whale as "folio" is ridiculously arbitrary, then, but it does point to the similar arbitrariness of the whale as "spouting fish with a horizontal tail"; both are remote from the whale—the supposed fact—with which we are concerned. Our response is reinforced when we consider that even the ostensibly easy task of classification by physical characteristics is given up, and the only consistent relation between words and whale in "Cetology" is as general and artificial as an aimless comparison with book sizes and a pseudodefinition from Ishmael's own dictionary. Our attention is specifically drawn, in this way, to the artificial nature of the language by which we are to know whales and Moby Dick. The cetological way of talking is practicable, Melville seems to say, and with it we can fabricate a neat verbal definition or a functional system of classification, but these definitions and systems are clearly arbitrary: we are dealing with words, not whales. And we are a long way from "the very pelvis of the world."

I do not mean to suggest that the attitudes displayed in "Cetology" are those to be found throughout the book, for considering the too easy confusions of the narrator and his whimsical tone, this chapter is a loaded case; but "Cetology" does provide a reader with a clue to a narrative technique that is pervasive in *Moby-Dick*: the exploitation of special and artificial kinds of language that serve to draw our attention to the limitations of such language and thus communicate in both a positive and a negative way: Moby Dick becomes both "a spouting fish with a horizontal tail" and all that must lie beyond the confines of this narrow perspective.

One may acquaint himself with this use of special languages in *Moby-Dick* simply by reviewing the titles of some of the chapters and noting the point of view that each chapter develops: "Cetology" (classifying), "The Advocate " (historical and eulogistic), "Fast Fish and Loose Fish" (legal), "Does the Whale Diminish" (naturalistic), "Monstrous Pictures of Whales," "Less Erroneous Pictures of Whales," "Of Whales in Paint, in Teeth, etc.," "The Whale as a Dish," "Measurement of the Whale's Skeleton," and "The Fossil Whale." This list is not exhaustive, and when we add to these essentially artificial ways of talking about whales all the technical accounts of the business and implements of whaling, which comprises a great special vocabulary in itself, we may have some notion of the manner in which much of this book is composed of internally consistent and singularly limited verbal systems. These special languages, again, are all similar in that their relevance to the central elements of the story, Ahab and Moby Dick, is remote, and while they combine to form an atmosphere of significances around the white whale and his pursuer, these significances serve primarily to emphasize their own limitations. A reader—aware of these limitations—is constantly preoccupied with the problem of penetrating beyond what he sees as sets of words to something more essential or, at least, more relevant. In this manner the special vocabularies of *Moby-Dick* communicate in primarily a negative manner; their imaginative limits are too obvious, and we must feel it necessary to go beyond them. They communicate, more than a sense of what Ahab and the white whale are, an awareness of what they are not.

The second sort of rhetorical pattern that I shall consider is the general counterpart of the "extracts" at the beginning of the book. It is the method of allusion, of reporting what someone else has said or might say about whales, whaling, and especially Moby Dick. Ishmael as the narrator makes use of this device continually and with various effects throughout the story, but it is usually most evident when his subject is important to himself and to a reader. The chapter entitled "Moby Dick" provides excellent examples.

Near the beginning of the chapter, Ishmael prepares us for what is to follow: "...the outblown rumors of the White Whale did in the end incorporate with themselves all manner of morbid hints, and half-formed foetal suggestions of supernatural agencies, which eventually invested Moby Dick with new terrors unborrowed from anything that visibly appears" (151). This is the narrator's sensible attitude; what he is considering is unquestioned superstition, and his tone is a mixture of contempt and relish. He alludes next to a specific source: "...we find some book naturalists—Olassen and Povelson—declaring the Sperm Whale not only to be a consternation to every other creature in the sea, but also to be so incredibly ferocious as continually to be athirst for human blood" (151). The relish is still there, of course, and the idea remains qualified by the fact that others have said it and by the narrator's unwillingness—for he subsequently labels it a superstition—to commit himself to it; it is not yet, strictly speaking, an accepted part of his story. And right whalemen have said, Ishmael continues, that "to chase and point lance at such an apparition as the Sperm Whale was not for mortal man. That to attempt it, would be inevitably to be torn into a quick eternity. On this head, there are some remarkable documents that may be consulted" (152). This statement, too, is presumably qualified, as the remark of someone else, but here Ishmael's refusal to commit himself in favor of the attitude is not so apparent; the last sentence, in fact, is surely ambiguous: what does "remarkable documents" mean? Are they remarkable for the superstitiousness they exhibit? For the documentary proof? The matter is open, and a reader is unsure whether or not the right whalemen's fantasy is to be regarded as a part of the literal narrative.

This technique of alluding to an attitude and refusing to commit himself for or against it is characteristic of Ishmael, and this would seem reasonable considering his obvious pleasure in employing the special vocabularies I have mentioned previously. He is at home in all vocabularies, and he often appears to recite them impartially and, it seems, for the sake of themselves. And like the special vocabularies, these reported attitudes usually remain as remote from a narrative commitment as is the context from which they come. The narrator almost never makes an unqualified remark, and a reader never knows what is essential to the story and what is not. He remains dissatisfied, then, but he nonetheless assimilates all the allusions and reports as part of an uncertain awareness of what sperm whales and Moby Dick might be.

This technique is partially explained in a passage that, for a reader, provides a welcome sort of solidity. The narrator begins with an obvious superstition: "One of the wild suggestings referred to, as at last coming to be linked with the White Whale in the minds of the superstitiously inclined, was the unearthly conceit that Moby Dick was ubiquitous." And yet as strong as "unearthly conceit" appears, this belief is not completely without support: "Nor, credulous as such minds must have been, was this conceit altogether without some faint show of superstitious probability. For as the secrets of the currents in the seas have never yet been divulged, even to the most erudite research..." (152). The endorsement is weak enough—"some faint show of superstitious probability"—and it is what follows that is most interesting as a clue to the narrator's method. We cannot know, we are told, what can happen beneath the sea; even the most "erudite research" has failed. This is the crucial point. The narrator continues with some historical data about encountering the same whale in distant places within a small amount of time, with the possibility of an undersea Northwest Passage, and with the fountain of Arethusa, but the first of these has little to do with real ubiquity, and the last two, in themselves, are just more qualified allusions. The contest was won when Ishmael declared that the "secrets of the currents" are undisclosed, that the ways of the whale remain "unaccountable to his pursuers"—when he asserted, in short, that we are dealing with the unfathomed, that available knowledge cannot tell us what we want to know. The narrator begins, then, with the doubtful possibility of ubiquity, yet when he says that the ways of the whale are secret, that no one knows, the scale of what is possible expands and, perhaps, disintegrates. He is now able to say that "these fabulous narrations are almost fully equalled by the realities of the whaleman" (153). Ishmael has a way out, of course, for "realities" might refer to the "real" historical data mentioned previously, but most readers, I think, will be persuaded of more.

The speaker has proceeded from "wild suggestings" to

19

"realities," and the method appears deceptively simple. He begins with the heavily qualified report of a superstition, of a literal impossibility; he then suggests that all is not known, and in this way the very criteria for what is possible or impossible are questioned: Ishmael establishes a world in which the fabulous might be the real, in which the figurative allusion might be the literal narrative itself.

I have attempted to show that, in one instance, Ishmael's willingness to admit the fabulous into his narrative depends upon his feeling that, in terms of the essentials of his story, he is dealing with the unknown. This feeling may also be relevant to the inclusion in the narrative of the many special vocabularies that I have mentioned previously, for when one is dealing with the unknown all vocabularies, no matter their specific shortcomings, are important. It is only in the case of these special languages, however, where the narrowness of the expressed perspective itself constitutes a statement of the limitations of this perspective, that Ishmael will speak literally and consistently. When he has prepared a reader for more significant narrative remarks, he articulates the qualifications that he has previously implied. Both the practice of including the clear and narrow literal vocabularies and that of employing the fabulous and expansive figurative allusions are, in this way, similarly motivated. Both arise out of the narrator's assumption that he is dealing with the unknown and out of his resultant refusal to venture a single, significant way of talking about it.

Ishmael's consequent suggestibleness—his willingness to adopt temporarily a fabulous view—may be seen in the following passage:

...it cannot be much matter of surprise that some whalemen should go still further in their superstitions, declaring Moby Dick not only ubiquitous, but immortal (for immortality is but ubiquity in time); that though groves of spears should be planted in his flanks, he would still swim away unharmed; or if indeed he should ever be made to spout thick blood, such a sight would be but a ghastly deception; for again in unensanguined billows hundreds of leagues away, his unsullied jet would once more be seen. (153)

We begin here, again, with a qualification, but once it has been made the narrator seems to be arguing for the superstition. His definition of "immortality" is perfectly apt and noncommittal in itself, but in context this remark seems part of a persuasive proof. The details of a hypothetical example of this immortality, furthermore, are anything but hypothetical; they are developed with an intensity and a finality that imparts to them a literal reality.

In terms of the logical qualifications of the passage, of course, Ishmael remains neutral, and the next sentence—when it labels Moby Dick's "immortality" as another of the "supernatural surmisings" surrounding him—apparently closes the issue. The imaginative intensity of the description itself, however, by which a hypothetical account seems part of the literal narrative, is evidence of Ishmael's inclination to devote himself imaginatively to all possibilities. This very imaginative willingness, as I have suggested, depends, paradoxically, upon the narrator's reluctance to commit himself in an unequivocal manner; it is because he is uncommitted that he may entertain the kind of attitude of which I have been speaking. He cannot violate a code of meanings for the white whale because he never establishes one vocabulary as more central than another. And this lack of commitment on his part in turn depends upon his most important verbal gesture: his repeated statements that the real essentials cannot be known.

In speculating upon the attitude of the "Pequod's" crew toward Moby Dick, the narrator remarks: "...what the White Whale was to them, or how to their unconscious understandings, also, in some dim, unsuspected way, he might have seemed the gliding great demon of the seas of life,—all this to explain, would be to dive deeper than Ishmael can go" (156). The narrative method that I have described is again apparent; the vagueness of the speculation and the uncertainty indicated in "might have seemed" are obvious. But "gliding great demon of the seas of life" partakes of an imaginative vitality that seems unqualified, and that becomes all the more significant when it is followed by Ishmael's admission that he cannot pursue the matter. The technique is characteristic; we are presented with a qualified but powerful suggestion regarding the white whale, and then, by virtue of the narrator's declaration that he cannot prove or disprove such an attitude, that he cannot, indeed, pursue it in any way, the matter remains open; the fabulous suggestion remains in its intensity before us as another possible meaning of those surrounding the white whale and as a statement of the narrator's inability. In order to demonstrate more clearly this connection between Ishmael's inability to know the essentials of his story and his repeated suggesting of supernatural possibilities, I shall now consider a third characteristic of the language of *Moby-Dick*: the speaker's use of figurative language that is both vague and mystical.

There was a "vague, nameless horror" about Moby Dick, Ishmael remarks in "The Whiteness of the Whale," "which at times by its intensity completely overpowered all the rest; and yet so mystical and well nigh ineffable was it, that I almost despair of putting it in a comprehensible form. It was the whiteness of the whale that above all things appalled me" (157). The despair mentioned here becomes apparent at crucial moments later in the chapter. At present the narrator continues with an extended account of the qualities of whiteness in the world, where it is associated with beauty, nobility, and, even, divinity. And yet, he declares, there "lurks an elusive something in the innermost idea of this hue, which strikes more of panic to the soul than that redness which affrights in blood" (158). We may note here that Ishmael's characterization of whiteness depends upon its elusiveness, that his account of it is founded not upon what it is, but upon what it is not or what it is more than. The method is perpetuated in what follows; the speaker continues, not with a closer consideration of possible definitions of whiteness, but with examples of various responses to the color: the terror inspired by the polar bear, the magical significance of the albatross, and the intrinsically repellent nature of the "albino man." The predominating method of this chapter, in fact, is the providing of examples of the power of whiteness and of many possible causes for this power, and with each example the essence of whiteness in relation to Moby Dick becomes more complex and more vague.

Near the end of the chapter the narrator admits his failure to solve, thus far, the "incantation of this whiteness," which is both the "symbol of spiritual things" and "the intensifying agent in things most appalling to mankind." He concludes the chapter with a passage that I shall quote in its entirety, for it is most revealing in terms of the matter with which I have to this point been concerned—Ishmael's narrative method:

Is it that by its indefiniteness it shadows forth the heartless voids and immensities of the universe, and thus stabs us from behind with the thought of annihilation, when beholding the white depths of the milky way? Or is it, that as in essence whiteness is not so much a color as the visible absence of color, and at the same time the concrete of all colors; is it for these reasons that there is such a dumb blankness, full of meaning, in a wide landscape of snows—a colorless, all-color of atheism from which we shrink? And when we consider that other theory of the natural philosophers, that all other earthly hues—every stately or lovely emblazoning—the sweet tinges of sunset skies and woods; yea, and the gilded velvets of butter-flies, and the butterfly cheeks of young girls; all these are but subtle deceits, not actually inherent in substances, but only laid on from without; so that all deified Nature absolutely paints like the harlot, whose allurements cover nothing but the charnel-house within, and when we proceed further, and consider that the mystical cosmetic which produces every one of her hues, the great principle of light, for ever remains white or colorless in itself, and if operating without medium upon matter, would touch all objects, even tulips and roses, with its own blank tinge—pondering all this, the palsied universe lies before us a leper; and like wilfull travellers in Lapland, who refuse to wear colored and coloring glasses upon their eyes, so the wretched infidel gazes himself blind at the monumental white shroud that wraps all the prospect around him. And of all these things the Albino whale was the symbol. Wonder ye then at the fiery hunt? (163)

We may notice that as Ishmael becomes more intensely concerned with his subject, his remarks increasingly take the form of questions and speculations—speculations of which the language is often strained and complex, with oxymorons like "a dumb blankness, full of meaning." The concluding sentences, like many throughout the chapter, are an allusion to another "theory," but their insistent tone is even more apparent than usual and commands our attention.

The speaker's emotional and intellectual attitudes are complicated here. His response to "Nature," for example, is dramatically ambivalent: she is at once "deified" and like a "harlot"; the deceptions she practices are both necessary and treacherous. And whiteness itself is something great and spiritual as well as that which transforms the universe into a "leper."

As complex as the narrator's thought is, however, a reader can make general sense of it when he considers its relation to Ishmael's manner of speaking as a whole. Ishmael is clearly convinced of a fundamental disparity in the world, a disparity between that which colors make apparent and that which whiteness would supposedly reveal, between appearance and essence, between natural forms and something like a "charnel-house" within them. Whiteness itself he sees as not a part of appearance or essence, but the means by which both are revealed; without the buffers of color and natural forms, whiteness displays the essence, and the universe is transformed.

And with all the confusions that the "Lapland travellers" simile evokes, one basic paradox remains dominant; whiteness is "a dumb blankness, full of meaning"; meaning is somehow connected with what would seem to be its antithesis, the absence of visible and audible form. This dichotomy between profundity and silence or meaning and blankness, of course, is not particularly illuminating in itself; it is a stock device in the literary imagination. When we consider, however, that we encounter this connection between meaning and blankness throughout *Moby-Dick* and that it may be seen, in general, to underly Ishmael's basic gestures as a narrator, it becomes significant. The genius of the sperm whale, the narrator remarks, "is declared in his doing nothing particular to prove it. It is moreover declared in his pyramidical silence" (273). And "seldom," he asserts in another passage, "have I known any profound being that had anything to say to this world" (290). The tone of these and many other examples, of course, is not consistent; Ishmael is often humorous, but the thought itself remains a prevailing one.

Closely related to this attitude are the narrator's frequent admissions of his inability to pursue the meaning of the story. We may consider the following passage: "Dissect him how I may, then, I but go skin deep; I know him not, and never will. But if I know not even the tail of this whale, how understand his head? much more, how comprehend his face?" (295) This attitude is both familiar and important, especially when we consider that it is simply the articulated synonym for Ishmael's constant failure to commit himself to a single perspective or vocabulary. This lack of commitment in itself composes a great series of statements to the effect that the essentials cannot be known. And because they cannot be known, infinite possibilities may be admitted. It is in this way that "silence" makes for "profundity."

But it is difficult to see Ishmael's multiple voices, even though they seem to be centerless, as a kind of silence. We may refer once again to the narrator's idea of whiteness as "the visible absence of color, and at the same time the concrete of all colors," as a "colorless, all-color of atheism." It should be clear that Ishmael's voice may be defined in precisely the same manner; it too is colorless because it is all color; Ishmael is voiceless because he is all voices. He surrounds the elements of the story with

special or technical language, with superstitious reports, allusions, and with figures of great imaginative intensity. And it is upon this very multiplicity of meaning that he finally relies; he refuses to limit himself to one way of speaking. A reader thus encounters in Ishmael many linguistic approaches to the story, all of which are indirect, all of which are possible, and none exclusive of other possibilities. This very suggestive but vacant multiplicity, again, corresponds exactly to the idea of whiteness itself—the "colorless, all-color," the "dumb blankness, full of meaning." It appears, then, that when whiteness—a crucial object of the narrator's perceptions—is defined, what has been defined is the means and manner of perception itself.

To clarify this matter it is important to remember that whiteness is the "mystical cosmetic" that operates from without upon natural "hues" that are also "laid on from without." Like whiteness in this respect, Ishmael's narrative method is always separable both from whatever lies beyond its particular "hues" and from the "hues" themselves, the verbal forms, the various ways of talking, that as a total method it employs and illuminates. And like whiteness, also, Ishmael's manner of speaking makes us aware of the "beyond"—the supposed reality—primarily in a negative way: we know that what it illuminates, the different "hues" or vocabularies whose form it variously takes, are "deceits."

In this manner Ishmael's attempts to define one of the fundamental subjects of his narrative take the form of a definition of his attempted manner of perception. The sought object cannot be identified; one can only say that this object is separable from the seeking and that it is only the seeking that can be known. Ishmael's own whiteness, his general impulse toward suggestive multiplicity, can only describe the "hues," the particular voices and vocabularies, which it initially creates.

We may paraphrase this attitude expressed in "The Whiteness of the Whale" as follows: Language can only illuminate itself; it is a deceit, a mask which continually and inevitably recreates itself in a permanent circularity, never reaching away from itself toward the reality, whatever that might be. It is perhaps the ultimate capacity of language and the final act of a narrator to define language itself as the focal subject of language and to perceive that this is in fact the ultimate linguistic act. And when Ishmael, for example, does so, he destroys as he must the value of verbal forms as perceptions of a reality. At this point he is left with language on the one hand and that which is beyond language on the other—with no connection between them. By means of whiteness he gazes upon whiteness; by means of language he defines only language. He contains all possibilities, but no single idea of what is real. He has, in other words, no "colored and coloring glasses" that might disguise the disparity between his languages and a reality. And in this way, like the Lapland traveller, Ishmael must be, at the most crucial moments, blind and dumb.

It is this many-voiced silence, this "dumb blankness, full of meaning," that comprises Ishmael's most important act of language, his response to the white whale itself. For Moby Dick is significant for him as the ultimate whiteness—that is, the sum of all the forms, the languages, the suggestive masks that he creates. In this way the whale is completely impenetrable to Ishmael; Moby Dick is a gigantic reflector from which his perceptions inevitably rebound upon themselves to emphasize their nature as remarks less relevant to the whale as the object of language than to the

qualities of language itself. Ishmael must treat the white whale as if it were the sum of all the language that he uses about the white whale; he knows that it is not, but to any other purpose his silence is enforced.

At this point we are far from a simple refusal on Ishmael's part to commit himself, or from a single instance of his declaring something to be unknown or in one set of terms unpursuable. The paradox here, I think, is that Ishmael's efforts seem significant largely because nothing is ever finally achieved. We are confronted with a multiplicity of languages, each of which is an example, often an imaginative and serious example, of a general inconclusiveness. The unknowns in the book increase in number and importance, and have their climax at such points as "The Whiteness of the Whale," where the movement of the narrator's language—and perhaps of all language—is shown to be inevitably circular. In this way the particular and personal "unknown" becomes the general and absolute "unknowable." Ishmael's failures, in their suggestiveness and ultimate inconclusiveness, become the evidence for the existence of what is beyond them, something expressed because it is not expressed, which we can only call the ineffable. This communication of the ineffable, however, is not only negative, for—although it depends upon the negation of Ishmael's imaginative efforts—his "failures" always work in two ways: to give partial form to what is beyond them and to assert that this form itself is artificial. The ineffable thus exists for a reader as a vast potential of significances which are irreducible, provisional, and unrealizable in any defined or final way.

It should be apparent at this point that the languages Ishmael employs, despite their various particularities, are in their rhetorical function equivalent. All begin with qualifications imposed by their nature as special vocabularies, reports, allusions, or, in general, as figures of speech, and all reflect the added limitation of Ishmael's refusal to commit himself to them. The final effect of all these languages, again, is to turn back upon themselves as artificial forms, as language, and in doing so to assert the existence of something ineffable beyond themselves. Previously I have used the word "mask" to describe these verbal forms, not only because this word suggests their artificiality, but also because the attitude that the word implies is central to the motivation and madness of Ahab, who exhibits his motives in the following passage:

Hark ye yet again,—the little lower layer. All visible objects, man, are but as pasteboard masks. But in each event—in the living act, the undoubted deed—there, some unknown but still reasoning thing puts forth the mouldings of its features from behind the unreasoning mask. If man will strike, strike through the mask! How can the prisoner reach outside except by thrusting through the wall? To me, the white whale is that wall, shoved near to me. Sometimes I think there's naught beyond. But 'tis enough. He tasks me; he heaps me; I see in him outrageous strength, with an inscrutable malice sinewing it. That inscrutable thing is chiefly what I hate; and be the white whale agent, or be the white whale principal, I will wreak that hate upon him. (139)

Immediately we may note Ahab's resemblances to Ishmael; he too is aware of a disparity between appearances and something beyond them. And although Ahab's appearances are expressed as "visible objects" whereas Ishmael's are generally characterized as language itself, the difference, in view of the correspondence between natural shapes and linguistic arrangements that I have mentioned earlier, seems slight. The linguistic and the visible are certainly equivalent, at any rate, with respect to their most important attribute here, their artificiality, their separableness from some "reality." We must note immediately, however, that it is only Ishmael's language that can be regarded as artificial at this point, for Ahab implies here, as he asserts later, that his own "language"—somehow connected with action—can penetrate beyond appearances. In this way his thought diverges from Ishmael's drastically; he admits, as does the narrator, that what lies behind the mask is unknown, even that it is inscrutable, but in the same breath he exhibits a fanatical certainty about it: it is a "reasoning thing," and what is "inscrutable" is its "malice"—not, of course, inscrutable at all. From this single example, it would appear that Ahab, in his feverish desire to commit himself upon what he declares is both unknowable and certain, is the opposite of Ishmael.

This poses the problem that is, I think, Melville's dominant concern in *Moby-Dick,* but the question of Ahab's motives and significance also presents a difficulty, for he too, like all else in the book, is subject to Ishmael's complex narrative flexibility. In the discussion that follows, however, I hope to show that many of the apparent inconsistencies in Ahab's characterization may be reconciled into a general pattern of Melville's intentions for him.

Melville displays these intentions at the outset, when Ishmael speculates upon the "fighting Quakers," the "Quakers with a vengeance" of Nantucket, and continues with what is surely a reference to Ahab. He speaks of "instances" of men "named with Scripture names" and "of greatly superior natural force, with a globular brain and a ponderous heart," and describes such a man as follows:

31

...who has also by the stillness and seclusion of many long night-watches in the remotest waters, and beneath constellations never seen here at the north, been led to think untraditionally and independently; receiving all nature's sweet or savage impressions fresh from her own virgin voluntary and confiding breast, and thereby chiefly, but with some help from accidental advantages, to learn a bold and nervous lofty language—that man makes one in a whole nation's census—a mighty pageant creature, formed for noble tragedies. Nor will it at all detract from him, dramatically regarded, if either by birth or other circumstances, he have what seems a half wilful overruling morbidness at the bottom of his nature. For all men tragically great are made so through a certain morbidness.... But as yet we have not to do with such an one, but with quite another....(75–76)

And in this manner we return to the matters of Peleg and Bildad.

Our expectations of Ahab are partially formed here. They involve, first, a man of heroic stature, who is not only characteristically a thinker but also an "untraditional" and "independent" thinker who has learned a "lofty language." Ishmael even suggests that *Moby-Dick* might end as a tragedy, and alludes to the "overruling morbidness" of Ahab which later is to be redefined and condemned as "monomania." A short time later Peleg speaks of Ahab, explicitly, as "ungodly" and "god-like," one who has "been used to deeper wonders than the waves; fixed his fiery lance in mightier, stranger foes than whales" (80). This clearly contains implications of the strangeness of Moby Dick, of the possibility that he is more than a whale, but it is also a metaphor, perhaps, and has to do with Ahab's having been "in colleges, as well as 'mong the cannibals." Again we have the suggestion that Ahab is an uncommon man who has experienced mysteries and whose stature, I think, is a stature of mind.

It may be added here that, even if the characterization of Ahab were finally inconsistent, the very fact that he is the central character in a narrative that is, as I have tried to show, fundamentally concerned with the powers of language would indicate that he is a dramatization of what is predominantly an imaginative problem. This is only true, of course, if Ishmael himself, as the narrator, is Ahab's superior in reliability—so that the imaginative difficulties he reveals may be taken as the fundamental problem of the narrative as a whole. And, also, it is only true if *Moby-Dick* is not two or more separable narratives, developing two or more distinct problems, but one. Of the former provision, there can be no question. The latter is in part dependent upon the analysis of the book that I am proposing.

Ahab's doctrine of masks, if we may call it that, resembles Ishmael's in its assertion of a split universe, of a disparity between the apparent and the real, and the captain of the "Pequod" seems even more concerned than Ishmael with apprehending something beyond the forms he sees as artificial. He speaks to a whale's head, for example, asking for the "secret thing" that is in it because it has "dived the deepest" (247), and the idea of great and unknown depths is often exhibited in the language that Ahab uses to describe his general course of action and thought. He insists that his "soul is grooved to run" over "unsounded gorges, through the rifled hearts of mountains, under torrents' beds" (142). He suggests constantly that he must proceed into and through the impenetrable and the unknown, while he is also aware that the unknown may not exist in a definable form, that it may be only the ineffable

33

itself, "imponderable thoughts" (339). Ahab, however, will not accept the imponderable as such; unlike Ishmael, whose inquiring intelligence begins and ends with language and the resulting suggestion of something ineffable beyond language, Ahab must go farther: "...but all the things that most exasperate and outrage mortal man, all these things are bodiless, but only bodiless as objects, not as agents" (424). Like the narrator of the book, Ahab is aware of something beyond artificial forms, but in him, again, this awareness takes shape as a positive, rather than as a largely negative, assertion. For to Ahab's mind there are "agents," and the supernatural can be revealed and embodied in the natural. It is precisely this sort of revelation that he sees, as the narrator suggests, in Moby Dick:

No turbaned Turk, no hired Venetian or Malay, could have smote him with more seeming malice...in his frantic morbidness he at last came to identify with him, not only all his bodily woes, but all his intellectual and spiritual exasperations. The White Whale swam before him as the monomaniac incarnation of all those malicious agencies which some deep men feel eating in them.... That intangible malignity which has been from the beginning; to whose dominion even the modern Christians ascribe one-half of the worlds; which the ancient Ophites of the east reverenced in their statue devil;—Ahab did not fall down and worship it like them; but deliriously transferring its idea to the abhorred white whale, he pitted himself, all mutilated, against it...all truth with malice in it...all evil, to crazy Ahab, were visibly personified, and made practically assailable in Moby Dick. (154)

To Ishmael the universal malice that Ahab perceives in the white whale is "seeming"—only possible as a suggestion—and though, as always, he lends himself imaginatively to Ahab's conception of Moby Dick, in the end he must employ an awkward, qualifying adjective: "all evil, to *crazy* Ahab."[2]

From the evidence thus far, then, it would appear that Ahab's position in terms of language and the possibilities of imaginative perception is antithetical to Ishmael's. For Ishmael the imagination begins and ends with language, and he is aware of the existence of something beyond his ordering imagination only in the sense that he fails to express it unequivocally. But what is ineffable for Ishmael is not so for Ahab; for him the world beyond the artifices of the visible—the supposed reality—is not unknowable but only unknown; it is potentially perceivable and, indeed, assailable through agents like the white whale—agents which, therefore, are themselves revelations. It is when both Ishmael and Ahab seem to display an awareness of these revelations that the narrator's characteristic appellation for Ahab—"monomaniac"—becomes most meaningful in terms of the narrative concerns I have discussed. When the shoals of small fish accompanying the outward-bound "Pequod" leave her for another ship, Ahab sees in this phenomenon a grim comment upon his own course of action, and Ishmael remarks, "to any monomaniac man, the veriest trifles capriciously carry meanings" (193). Ishmael himself, as the narrator, has made suggestive use of the incident, but he nonetheless condemns Ahab's interpretation of it, which is only unlike his own implication in that it is final; it implies no awareness of its artificialty as an interpretation. Ahab reads the event clearly and unequivocally, and his reading, for Ishmael, is only one of the things that one might say about the event; in his insistence that the "trifle" is the "meaning," and admits

[2]My italics.

no other, Ahab becomes for the narrator a "monomaniac." This is not to say, of course, that the term as Ishmael uses it always has this meaning, but only that—even though this word is also used to describe an insanity suggested to be less complex—it is often associated with the vision of the world that I have remarked, because this vision is for Ishmael beyond the limits of the indubitably sane.

Much later in the book, Starbuck and Ahab view the captain's boat, which has been smashed by Moby Dick; the first mate declares it is an "omen," and Ahab responds with a wonderful outburst: " 'Omen? omen?—the dictionary! If the gods think to speak outright to man, they will honorably speak outright; not shake their heads, and give an old wives' darkling hint.—Begone!' " (416). We may make use of Ahab's definition of "omen" in considering Ishmael's narrative method, for in Ahab's terms this method is indeed one great "omen," composed as it is of intense but ambiguous and qualified suggestions, which might define an essential reality, but do not. For Ahab, however, the creation and perception of suggestions are not the limits of imagination; it is possible and even necessary for the "gods" to "speak outright," for something more real than an ambiguous tension between artificial forms and what might be beyond them to reveal itself through these forms. We should not feel, that is to say, that Ishmael condemns Ahab because the latter presumes to prescribe the functions of the gods or presumes himself the object of these functions, for Ishmael implies elsewhere that, were revelation the unquestioned work of deities, Ahab would be the kind of man to whom such revelations would be made. Ahab's presumption, his mania, seems rather to lie in his certainty of a perceivable and unambiguous world order, in which there are gods who reveal unequivocal truth.

If we were to reduce this relation between Ishmael and Ahab, in short, to a grammatical definition, we might say that for Ishmael the imagination may deal with the objects of imagination only by means of suggestive approximations that are always qualified to be approximations, and that the relation of the resultant imaginative order to the object is precisely the relation of the simile to its object, in that the meaning may exist only as inseparable from and dependent upon its qualifiedness. In the practice of Ahab, the contemplated object becomes the meaning which the imagination provides; meaning is embodied in the object, and becomes the reality that one may perceive in what was previously an artificial mask. Ahab's position is that of the seer, then, whose imaginative perceptions of the world become the reality of the world. And the relation between the perceived reality and the object in which it is perceived can only be called metaphorical or symbolic. As a theory of language, it is antithetical to Ishmael's sense of the artificiality of the verbal and of the existence of the ineffable; as a vision it is, for Ishmael, insanity.

The narrator's implicit position, as I have suggested, is always flatly opposed to Ahab's; his explicit views, however, are often more complicated. They comprehend, first, a body of somewhat ambiguous warnings like the description of the masthead stander who "takes the mystic ocean at his feet for the visible image of that deep, blue, bottomless soul, pervading mankind and nature...every dimly-discovered, uprising fin of some undiscernible form, seems to him the embodiment of those elusive thoughts that only people the soul by continually flitting through it" (136). While in this fit of pantheism and lost "identity,"

Ishmael continues, the man may slip; his "identity" will return, and he may fall headlong into the sea and perish: "Heed it well, ye Pantheists!" The masthead stander is at least generally analogous to Ahab in that he sees in visible things the "embodiment" of what Ahab himself, somewhat later, will term "imponderable thoughts," but the admonitory prophecy of death for the masthead stander is intensified with respect to Ahab when we consider that for the former an awareness of the ineffable is dependent upon the visible forms themselves remaining "undiscernible." The masthead stander's "visible images" are not really images, and reality, like its vague embodiment, is formless; the ineffable is perhaps recognized as such. The images in which Ahab perceives reality, however—Moby Dick himself, for example—are sharply outlined in his view, and in them he defines the "imponderable" unambiguously. But even though the masthead stander's identification with the ineffable might seem partly redeemed by its vagueness, it is nonetheless reckless, for if in the midst of this vision he regains his "identity"— if he realizes, I think, the nature of the separation between his imagination and reality, the separation that he has attempted to bridge—he falls. Ishmael's narrative method, of course, reveals his unwillingness to bridge such a gap, his conviction that to attempt to do so would be both futile and disastrous. His imaginative "leaps" take the form of qualified movements from one vocabulary to another, always recognizing the artificiality of each and thus retaining his "identity." His words are tentative, experimental probes into the universe and the self, which never result in a "pantheism" or in the vaguest sort of conviction, but in a deprivation of belief, signified in a

word like "atheism"—a multiple, suggestive, and centerless atheism.[3]

In other instances, Ishmael's admonitions to a reader
assert the value, perhaps even the necessity, of Ahab's
dangerous perspective: "For unless you own the whale, you
are but a provincial and sentimentalist in Truth. But clear
Truth is a thing for salamander giants only to encounter;
how small the chances for the provincials, then? What befel
the weakling youth lifting the dread goddess's veil at
Sais?" (267) It is suggested here that "clear Truth" is
ultimate truth, and we may note that if anyone in *Moby-
Dick* approaches the nature of a "salamander giant," it
is Ahab in all his explicit connections with fire. Ishmael,
however, later seems to deny that this "Truth" is desirable
or, indeed, that it is truth: "But even Solomon, he says,
'the man that wandereth out of the way of understanding
shall remain' (*i.e.* even while living) 'in the congregation
of the dead.' Give not thyself up, then, to fire, lest it invert
thee, deaden thee" (328). The warning in context is to

[3]Walter E. Bezanson describes a similar distinction between Ishmael and Ahab. Of the more important metaphors of the narrative
he remarks that "their meanings are not single but multiple; not
precisely equatable but ambiguous; not more often reinforcing than
contradictory. The symbolism of *Moby-Dick* is not static but is in
motion. . . ." Bezanson characterizes Ahab as one who "increasingly
reduces all pluralities to the singular. . . . His destruction follows
when he substitutes an allegorical fixation for the world of symbolic
potentialities." "*Moby-Dick*: Work of Art," in *Moby-Dick Centennial
Essays,* ed. Tyrus Hillway and Luther S. Mansfield (Dallas: Southern
Methodist University Press, 1953), pp. 47, 48. In a more pejorative
comment, Richard Chase agrees with this conception of Ahab: "The
true hero commits himself to the rhythms of life and achieves a
creative mobility among extremes. The false hero is he who cannot
achieve this mobility but commits himself, not to the tensions and
harmonies within extremes, but to the extremes themselves." *Herman
Melville: A Critical Study* (New York: Macmillan Co., 1949), p. 137.

the reader, for Ishmael has become confused by gazing at
the fire in the try-works, but it has also a specific relevance
to Ahab, to the "salamander giant."

One may well ask that if Ahab's course is suggested to
be a superhuman path toward "clear Truth" and also to be
"out of the way of understanding," what is truth or reality
in *Moby-Dick*? And at this point it is necessary to realize
that there is perhaps not one kind of truth in the book,
but—at least until the issues are finally resolved—two.
There is the clear and perilous "Truth" of "salamander
giants"—and we may note that in this conjunction Ahab's
vision of things is potentially the ultimate reality—and
there is Ishmael's truth, which he in part defines in the
following passage: "But as in landlessness alone resides the
highest truth, shoreless, indefinite as God—so, better is it
to perish in that howling infinite, than be ingloriously
dashed upon the lee, even if that were safety" (99)! Only
part of this is relevant, for neither Ahab nor Ishmael are
concerned with the "safety" of the "lee."[4] The "highest
truth" mentioned here is obviously not "clear Truth,"
but its opposite, something associated with "landlessness"
and particularly with the "indefinite"; it is analogous, I
think, to Ishmael's suggestive but qualified manner of
speaking, in which a reader becomes aware of the inexpressible. It is opposed, again, to the harsh clarity of Ahab's
vision of a definable reality and his faith in a single kind of
language. In the indirectness and indefiniteness of Ish-

[4]Perhaps this "safety" might be that of an ignorance, either in-
voluntary or willed, that would accept an artificial vocabulary as real,
the safety of a mind that would not be or would choose not to be
aware of the limitations of language. It is a man like this, perhaps,
whom Marlow describes in "Heart of Darkness" as "too much of a
fool to go wrong—too dull even to know you are being assaulted by
the powers of darkness."

mael's truth, and in its assumption that reality can only be expressed suggestively and negatively as the incommunicable, this is the highest truth possible, as the narrator sees it, for the human imagination. We are all, to Ishmael's mind, "provincials."

In his attempts at "clear Truth," then, Ahab is more ambitious than Ishmael, whose language functions to display its insufficiency. If the arguments ended here then *Moby-Dick* might well be the tragedy of a Promethean figure who must die because the quality of his imagination exceeds the limits of his universe; Ahab would be destroyed because in his progress toward a symbolic revelation of Ishmael's ineffable reality he outraged the imaginative conventions that the narrator has created in the universe of *Moby-Dick;* the whole world would be against him. Ahab might then be seen as a dramatization of a possible sort of imaginative perception whose mortal struggle to know the supposed unknowable would be unquestionably heroic. But complications arise.

If Ahab's course of action is a metaphysical attempt to define the undefinable, it is also a simple struggle for revenge. While his vision in perceiving the white whale as the incarnation of evil and supernatural malice possibly involves a step beyond the limits upon which Ishmael insists—and thus seems an insanity if we are to say that the narrator is sane—it is also the product of a simpler insanity, for as a vision it is limited to one revelation, one symbol. Moby Dick is Evil, and Ahab does not look elsewhere. This is not, perhaps, as serious a limitation as one might think, for Ishmael's own suggestions of what the ineffable might be frequently have connotations of evil, but it is a limitation.

The symbolic perception and the vengeful blindness,

furthermore, are inseparable, not only because both are in Ishmael's terms insanity, but also because they are more generally treated so throughout the book. The meaningful vision of the whale does not exist independently of the motive for vengeance; the vengeance is not pursued independently of the vision which gives it meaning. We may also remember, in this connection, that even in his suggestive speech on the "masks," Ahab implies that action is at least as important to him as language; this might involve an assumption of action itself as unambiguous language, of course, but it also seems likely that it is closely connected with Ahab's desire for revenge.

Vision and revenge remain inseparable to the last; Ahab's mortal encounter with the whale does not define the preponderance of one over the other. He can die only once, and the enraged whale is just as deadly as the perception of a reality, which Ishmael is convinced must remain ineffable, might be. In one respect, certainly, Ahab's nature as a seer is seriously questioned, for it depends upon a kind of perceptiveness that in *Moby-Dick* has been seen to be both impossible and supernatural, and when Ahab is at the point of death he is deprived of any supernatural aspect.

Unquestionably, Ahab's death is the most important element in his story. It may be seen as Melville's final metaphorical statement that all language—even Ahab's— is artificial, that the ineffable must exist as such, that its reality cannot be perceived. In this last instance Melville need not employ Ishmael to say, "I can go no farther"; the death of Ahab is the culmination of all the various expressions in *Moby-Dick* of man's inability to perceive what is beyond the artifices of perception.

Ishmael displays his awareness of the enforced circularity of his own imaginative course when he wishes the world "an endless plain" so that "by sailing eastward we could forever reach new distances." "But," he continues, "in pursuit of those far mysteries we dream of, or in tormented chase of that demon phantom that, some time or other, swims before all human hearts; while chasing such over this round globe, they either lead us on in barren mazes or midway leave us whelmed" (194). In considering Ahab's death we must see a distinction between the two last alternatives in this passage. It is Ishmael and the reader who have been led on in "mazes," but it is Ahab who is "whelmed." For Melville both employs Ahab's death as the failure of his insistent search and presents the death to a reader as an enigma—it is the last element of the maze. Like an example of Ishmael's language, Ahab has existed as an intense imaginative possibility, a potential perception—qualified by his own mania for revenge—of the ineffable. When he disappears, strangling and soundless, beneath the surface of the sea, the matter of vision is left open, for the question in a reader's mind is not whether one dies in perceiving the ineffable, but whether it has in fact been perceived. Ahab's death does not answer this question but sustains it. The death becomes Melville's insistence upon Ahab's course as only another potential meaning of which we cannot know the issue. Like the white whale to Ishmael, it is a barrier that a reader cannot penetrate, a reflecting wall that turns our inquiries back upon themselves; possibilities remain possibilities.

Ahab's failure is the metaphorical culmination of all Ishmael's suggestive failures; like those failures, it does not destroy possibilities but sustains them. The paradox here is one that I have suggested is the predominating paradox of *Moby-Dick* itself. Ahab's violent failure transforms what might have been the ultimate perception into the ultimate approximation; his imaginative course becomes in his death the last language of the many languages of the book that exist as possibilities because they fail as definitions. The irony is thus grim, for Ahab insists upon one sort of language only to become the implement of the other. But as do the failures of all these languages, Ahab's failure constitutes the success of *Moby-Dick*; the very evidence of impenetrability suggests a vague significance; a reader becomes aware of something ineffable that is opposed and surrounded by suggestive rhetoric insufficient to define it. The "dumb blankness" is "full of meaning."

The death of Ahab is revealing, I think, regarding the author's relation to his narrator and to his central character—Melville's relation to Ishmael and Ahab—a serious question, in itself, in *Moby-Dick*. For this death is most clearly part of the story that Melville has created; it is a dramatic moment that does not depend, as a moment, upon Ishmael's figures and qualifications, even though it is finally colored by them. When we consider that the death functions in such a way as to transform Ahab's imaginative direction into that of Ishmael, into the very sort of language that Ishmael employs throughout *Moby-Dick,* we may see it as Melville's endorsement of the attitude toward language and the ineffable that his narrator has held throughout the book.

This is to say that finally we may under no circumstances conceive of Ishmael and Ahab as the poles of Melville's imagination, or, considering its conclusion, see *Moby-Dick* as a dramatic working out of a real problem in Melville's mind. If Melville has maintained a detachment from his narrator somewhat similar to his detachment from

44

Ahab—in that both are active characters with names who seem to go their own way unattended by another consciousness—Ahab's death functions to dissolve this detachment and close the imaginative gap between author and narrator. It is of course beyond doubt that Melville entertains the possibility of Ahab's symbolic vision and language, but it is also clear that he entertains it only to demonstrate that it is impossible.

And here we may find a clue to the ambiguous and unsatisfying aspects of the death itself. Ahab's death is neither specifically tragic nor generally meaningful in the framework he has himself created for it, for Ahab himself has not been accepted on his own terms. He threatens to perceive the ineffable—and here perception is inseparable from revenge, and the mad seer inseparable from the mad fool. And the failure of the attempt becomes the corroboration of Ishmael's point of view and is in fact assimilated perfectly into Ishmael's vision of the world: far from constituting an independent and real language, Ahab's position is only another suggestion that is shown to fail, that can only exist as imaginative potential and artifice. But Ahab and, occasionally, Ishmael have insisted that Ahab must stand for more than this, and because his position finally can only be less significant than he has declared, Ahab, unlike Prometheus, is shown to be wrong. In this manner he is not a tragic hero who struggles with the gods of Ishmael's imagination with Melville looking on, but a kind of ritual sacrifice to those gods. And because only Melville is responsible for this, Ishmael's gods are Melville's gods. The ineffable of Ishmael is the ineffable of *Moby-Dick,* and the difference between author and narrator—as a reader has perhaps suspected all along—is only nominal.

45

CHAPTER III

"*Heart of Darkness*"
The Failure of Imagination

"HEART OF DARKNESS" is apparently an account of one man's moral and psychological degeneration and of another's spatial and intellectual journey to understand the essentials of the matter. A reader expects that such a story will follow certain rules: the journey will be difficult, but at its end will be a meaningful disclosure in which the "degeneration" will be placed in a moral framework. I shall try to show in this discussion, however, that "Heart of Darkness" may be seen to deny, particularly, the relevance of such a moral framework and to question, generally, the possibilities of meaning for the journey itself—that as the narrative develops it is redefined so as to deny the basic assumptions upon which it appears to be constructed.

One of the two possible assertions of the title is this: the "darkness" has a "heart"; a reader penetrates the unknown and the partially known to the known. Marlow suggests throughout the story that at the center of things there is meaning and that he is pursuing this meaning. And yet the intensity of Marlow's inquiries serves only to emphasize the inconclusiveness of his findings. Again and again he seems about to declare the truth about Kurtz and the darkness, but his utterances most often take form in either a thunderous contradiction in terms or a hushed and introspective bemusement. In this manner we are left with the second and possibly the dominant assertion of the title in particular and "Heart of Darkness" in general: it is the "heart," above all, that is composed of "darkness," there that the real darkness lies, and our progress must be through the apparently or partially known to the unknown.

The paradox implied in the title is nowhere more obvious than at what is usually taken to be the center of the story: Kurtz's deathbed cry, "The horror! The horror!"[1] These words seem a response to the most private nightmare, to the unknown itself, but Marlow insists that they are quite the reverse: a "moment of complete knowledge." He asserts that "the horror" has to do not only with Kurtz's unspeakable history, but also with the world at large, "wide enough to embrace the whole universe, piercing enough to penetrate all the hearts that beat in the darkness" (151). In attempting to resolve this apparent contradiction, we may inquire into what can be known of Kurtz's history.

Once he was an idealist of a kind, a member of the "new gang of virtue" of the trading company, and, according to Marlow, a man who apparently "had come out equipped with moral ideas of some sort" (88). A complication of this view of Kurtz as a moral man is presented near

---

[1] Joseph Conrad, "Heart of Darkness," *The Works of Joseph Conrad,* 20 vols. (London and Edinburgh: John Grant, 1925), VI, 149. All subsequent references to "Heart of Darkness" are to this edition. The edition of Conrad's works cited here will be referred to hereafter as "Conrad, *Works.*"

the end of the story by a sometime journalist colleague: " 'He electrified large meetings. He had faith—don't you see?—he had the faith' " (154). From the journalist's account to this point, a reader might be inclined to accept the possible but oversimple view of Kurtz as a clear case of moral degeneration; the man once possessed "the faith," which a reader may infer to be some high-minded and unambiguous creed, and then, in Africa, lost "the faith." Kurtz would have fallen, in these terms, within the framework of a traditional moral scheme, from a "heaven" to a "hell." But as the journalist continues, his description turns upon itself: " '...the faith. He could get himself to believe anything—anything. He would have been a splendid leader of an extreme party.' 'What party?' I asked. 'Any party,' answered the other. 'He was an—an—extremist.' Did I not think so? I assented." Kurtz is characterized as a man who possessed all faiths, or any faith. Marlow, like a reader, momentarily does not understand this and asks, "What party?"—implying that he too conceives "the faith" as a single moral ideal to which Kurtz dedicated himself. But then the matter becomes clearer; "the faith" is some quality or ability that enabled Kurtz to believe in any creed whatsoever. With this assessment Marlow agrees.

The problem of the connection between Kurtz's eloquent and unscrupulous moral facility and Kurtz himself—his essential being—concerns Marlow more than any other. On the last stage of the voyage up the river to the Inner Station, with the blood of his "second-rate helmsman" in his shoes, he reflects this concern in a feeling of disappointment, as though the man he is seeking were "something altogether without a substance." Marlow imagines Kurtz not "as doing, you know, but as discoursing"; it is Kurtz's voice alone that is the man's "real presence," "his ability to talk, his words" (113). Even after the actual, physical shock of Kurtz's appearance and, finally, of his death, Marlow insists, "The voice was gone. What else had been there? But I am of course aware that next day the pilgrims buried something in a muddy hole" (150). The pilgrims buried an anonymous "something," as if Kurtz's reality were completely detached from Kurtz as defined by his voice.

The separation between Kurtz's speech and Kurtz's unvoiced self is often described in relation to his "degeneration." As Marlow contemplates the human heads upon posts near Kurtz's station, he remarks that "they only showed that Mr. Kurtz lacked restraint in the gratification of his various lusts, that there was something wanting in him—some small matter which, when the pressing need arose, could not be found under his magnificent eloquence" (131). The "whisper" of the wilderness "echoed loudly within him because he was hollow at the core." It is thus suggested that Kurtz found himself in a world which—in comparison to civilization with its externally imposed restraints of law, social morality, and public opinion—was a world of enticing and dangerous possibilities, where a man must depend upon his "own innate strength," his "power of devotion...to an obscure back-breaking business" (116–117). Kurtz had no such devotion; his capacity for arbitrary eloquence and belief left him "hollow at the core." "The faith," we may now suppose, was Kurtz's faith in himself, not as a moral being but as a being who could use or discard morality. Kurtz lived as if what was most essential about him were wholly separate from what he professed to believe. But this, Marlow insists, is not simply hypocrisy: "...I had to deal with a being to whom I could not appeal in the name of anything high or low. I had, even like the niggers, to invoke him—himself—his own exalted and incredible degradation. There was nothing either above or below him, and I knew it. He had kicked himself loose of the earth. Confound the man! he had kicked the very earth to pieces" (144). Kurtz's "degradation" is not the traditional result of a moral failure; it is "exalted and incredible," perhaps godlike; it is the effect of his setting himself apart from the earth and the morality of the earth—apart, even, from the language of the earth with which he had such magnificent facility.

What Kurtz has done has general consequences. He has detached himself from the moral world, but in doing so he has, at least for Marlow, destroyed that world. Not simply has he "kicked himself loose of the earth," but "kicked the very earth to pieces." Kurtz's personal amorality has public ramifications, and Marlow is shaken; he declares—looking ahead to Kurtz's "the horror!"—that "no eloquence could have been so withering to one's belief in mankind as his final burst of sincerity" (145). "Belief in mankind," I think, implies the moral nature of mankind, the very business in which Kurtz could be so adept, and in releasing himself from this moral nature, Kurtz has illustrated not only the possibility of such a release but also, as Marlow suggests, the possible inadequacy and irrelevance of morality to all men. Kurtz's "failure" thus becomes his achievement, and if that achievement remains partially a failure, the adequacy of moral codes is nonetheless questioned.

This problem is a familiar one to readers of Conrad. The imaginative, moral man enters a world of danger and enticement; he struggles, alone, to retain his morality. Often he fails. But in "Heart of Darkness" the matter is more complicated, for here the possible moralities, the means of restraint, may be seen to be less available—as alternatives, unreal. I have attempted to show something of the manner in which morality may be seen to fail Kurtz in "Heart of Darkness"; what follows is an account of the failure of morality in more pervasive terms.

Throughout the story a reader is confronted with various kinds of "restraint" that are clearly unsatisfactory. The chief accountant "accomplishes something" with his fastidious dress, for example, and the manager masks his envious and continual deceit with a hypocritical concern for saying and doing "the right thing." The most obvious case of this false kind of discipline is Marlow's native helmsman; he "thought all the world of himself. He was the most unstable kind of fool I had ever seen. He steered with no end of a swagger while you were by; but if he lost sight of you, he became instantly the prey of an abject funk, and would let that cripple of a steamboat get the upper hand of him in a minute" (109).

In addition to these pseudomoralities, there are men for whom restraint is unnecessary: "...you may be too much of a fool to go wrong—too dull even to know you are being assaulted by the powers of darkness.... Or you may be such a thunderingly exalted creature as to be altogether deaf and blind to anything but heavenly sights and sounds" (116–117). None of these responses to the wilderness is possible for Marlow, nor, to Marlow's mind, for Kurtz. Both are men to whom the simpler falsehoods as morality do not appeal, and each, of course, possesses sufficient imagination to render him dangerously vulnerable to the "darkness."

Marlow declares that in confronting the wilderness, the "truth" of it, a man must "meet that truth with his own true stuff—with his own inborn strength. Principles won't do. Acquisitions, clothes, pretty rags—rags that would fly off at the first good shake. No; you want a deliberate belief" (97). At this point Marlow's conception of restraint sounds fine indeed. He continues, asserting that when the wilderness appealed to him—as it must to every man—he had a "voice" of his own. Immediately following his testimonial to his own "voice," however, he admits that what prevented him from going "ashore for a howl and a dance" was only that he was too busy keeping his steamboat in one piece: "I had to mess about with white-lead...watch the steering, and circumvent those snags.... There was surface-truth enough in these things to save a wiser man" (97). Marlow's ideal, as the kind of "truth" that a man may use to defend himself against the "truth" of the wilderness, is only a practical concern; it is founded upon keeping oneself busy, upon attending to matters of the surface.

Marlow says at one moment that it is in "work" that a man may "find" himself, his own "reality" (85); later, however, he appears to contradict himself and remarks, "When you have to attend to things of that sort, to the mere incidents of the surface, the reality—the reality, I tell you—fades. The inner truth is hidden—luckily, luckily. But I felt it all the same" (93). As these quotations indicate, Marlow uses the term "reality" in two ways: the primary reality is the suggested essence of the wilderness, the darkness that must remain hidden if a man is to survive morally, while the secondary reality is a figurative reality like work, an artificial reality by which the truly real is concealed or even replaced. And Marlow admits that this reality of the second sort is simply a deluding activity, a fictitious play over the surface of things.

Marlow's account of his own restraint as a fiction reflects his nature as a "wanderer"; he is as morally rootless, perhaps, as Kurtz himself. In speaking of the "droll thing life is," Marlow describes his difficulties in a way that is sug gestive in terms of Kurtz's experience:

I have wrestled with death. It is the most unexciting contest you can imagine. It takes place in an impalpable grayness, with nothing underfoot, with nothing around, without spectators, without clamour, without glory, without the great desire of victory, without the great fear of defeat, in a sickly atmosphere of tepid skepticism, without much belief in your own right, and still less in that of your adversary. If such is the form of ultimate wisdom, then life is a greater riddle than some of us think it to be. (150–151)

Marlow suggests that at certain moments—in struggling with death or, perhaps, with a wilderness—it is most difficult for a man to see any reality in a connection between moral "rights" and his experience; a man's most severe challenges are necessarily encountered in an "atmosphere of tepid skepticism." When Marlow himself struggles to keep the steamer afloat, struggles for his life, he replaces his own "tepid skepticism" with work; he is forced to do so by his physical danger. Kurtz's situation has by no means been so simple. Like Marlow, he had no dominating or saving "idea," but neither did he have Marlow's physical danger with its consequent activity—the work that luckily hides the reality.

In this manner Kurtz appears even more vulnerable than Marlow. For him the "tepid skepticism" was more intense; he viewed the disparity between his moral fictions and an amoral reality more starkly. Why he necessarily did so, I have considered only in part, but if we are to rely at all upon Marlow's insistence that Kurtz's experience corresponds to his own, then we may conclude for the moment that Kurtz's act of "kicking himself loose of the earth" was caused by his inability to save himself with fictions; when Kurtz's vision—the vision which Marlow assumes to be so similar to his own—destroyed the truth of morality and restraint, it also destroyed their availability.

It is on this account, I think, that Marlow refuses to condemn Kurtz in a moral way. The manager of the company remarks that Kurtz's "method" is "unsound," but Marlow denies this, asserting that it is "no method at all" (137–138). The manager conceives that Kurtz *was* once a "remarkable man" when his method was sound, perhaps, but that since then he has gone wrong. Talk of "sound" or "unsound" is irrelevant for Marlow, however, and Kurtz *is* a "remarkable man" exactly because he has escaped the world of sound and unsound, because he has shown that such terms are inadequate as a measure of his experience. Kurtz's crime or achievement, then, is not that he has managed things badly for the company or, more generally, that he has sinned in a uniquely horrifying way, but that by means of an act of vision he has cut himself off from the possibility of sin. At the moment of this conversation with the manager, Marlow formally declares his sympathy with Kurtz.

Throughout "Heart of Darkness," again, it is not simply the codes of the minor characters that are shown to be ignoble, nor is it only Marlow's code that is proved a tenuous fiction. Discipline in general is defined in the story not only as restraint, but also as a singleness of idea or intention—in contrast, of course, to something like Kurtz's multiple "faith" or to the infinite possibilities of the wilderness. This kind of spiritual rigidity is the important quality of the book which Marlow finds on his way to the Inner Station—"*An Inquiry into some Points of Seamanship*": "Not a very enthralling book; but at the first glance you could see there a singleness of intention, an honest concern for the right way of going to work.... The simple old sailor, with his talk of chains and purchases, made me forget the jungle and the pilgrims in a delicious sensation of having come upon something unmistakably real" (99). The "reality" of the book, its single-minded concern with work, is clearly the artificial or secondary reality that I have remarked, but it is more interesting to note here that when such reality seems possible, it seems so only in terms that are anomalous in the wilderness. It is apparent that this book is totally out of place in the jungle, that despite Marlow's desperate grasp on the book as a symbol of moral reality, this reality is rendered false and unreal by means of the very quality by which he declares it established: its irrelevance to the wilderness surrounding it.

In a similar manner, the wilderness may be seen elsewhere to deny singleness of purpose or, its equivalents, restraint and morality. As Marlow proceeds down the coast at the beginning of his journey, he encounters a French gunboat firing into the jungle:

There wasn't even a shed there, and she was shelling the bush. It appears the French had one of their wars going on thereabouts. Her ensign dropped limp like a rag; the muzzles of the long six-inch guns stuck out all over the low hull; the greasy, slimy swell swung her up lazily and let her down, swaying her thin masts. In the empty immensity of earth, sky, and water, there she was, incomprehensible, firing into a continent. Pop, would go one of the six-inch guns; a small flame would dart and vanish, a little white smoke would disappear, a tiny projectile would give a feeble screech—and nothing happened. Nothing could happen. (61–62)

War, with its polarities of life and death, victory and

defeat, enemy and enemy, may be seen generally as a straightforward matter. Guns, too, are traditionally and rigidly purposeful, and when they are fired something ought to happen. Here nothing happens: the guns "pop"; the projectiles are "feeble"; there is no enemy and no result. In a parallel description, explosives are used at the first station to remove a cliff: "The cliff was not in the way or anything; but this objectless blasting was all the work going on" (64). The blasting is not only "objectless," but also without effect, for "no change appeared on the face of the rock." A moment later Marlow sees six natives—"criminals"—in chains, hears another explosion, and then synthesizes these phenomena with his recollection of the gunboat:

Another report from the cliff made me think suddenly of that ship of war I had seen firing into a continent. It was the same kind of ominous voice; but these men could by no stretch of imagination be called enemies. They were called criminals, and the outraged law, like the bursting shells, had come to them, an insoluble mystery from the sea. (64)

The law—with its apparent, straightforward purpose—like the shells and the blasting has been negated; it has become a mystery, incomprehensible, and has no effect as law, but merely renders the savages indifferent and unhappy. Here the law, the blasting, and the warfare, then, are characterized as having no disciplined purpose or effect, and the disparity between these devices of civilization and the wilderness which they attempt corresponds to the disparity between morality and the wilderness mentioned previously. The scope of this disparity between human schemes and the wilderness, as we proceed through the story, is ever widening.

It has been remarked here that Marlow's own capacity for restraint in Africa depends upon his busy thoughtlessness, and he has said that this restraint reflects a concern only with the incidents of the surface, as opposed to the "reality" at the heart. The narrator who begins "Heart of Darkness" defines Marlow's manner of storytelling in a way that is puzzling yet clearly analogous to Marlow's own characterizations of his moral attitude:

The yarns of seamen have a direct simplicity, the whole meaning of which lies within the shell of a cracked nut. But Marlow was not typical...and to him the meaning of an episode was not inside like a kernel but outside, enveloping the tale which brought it out only as a glow brings out a haze, in the likeness of one of these misty halos that sometimes are made visible by the spectral illumination of moonshine. (48)

In "Heart of Darkness" we observe Marlow moving along the coast of the wilderness or over the surface of the river, and here we encounter the idea of his language moving over the outside of an "episode," surrounding the episode but never penetrating it. Marlow's attempts at meaning in general, then, take the same form as his attempts at morality in particular. Both meaning and morality are seen to be matters of the surface or exterior, while the reality—not Marlow's artificial reality but the reality beyond surfaces—is something deep within, something at the center that is not approached. There is an important difference, however, between Marlow's moral attitudes and his more generally meaningful attitudes: in the first instance he continually suggests that it would be imprudent to look beneath the surface; in the second he just as frequently admits that it is impossible to do so.

The emphasis of the passage quoted above is affirmative; the narrator implies that the search for meaning can be satisfied, somehow, in a concern with the exterior. And yet the very structure of "Heart of Darkness"—with the journey to the Inner Station, toward the man who constitutes the end of the search, and, certainly, toward some meaning in terms of the pervasive metaphor of "meaning at the heart"—seems to assert that there is a more significant reality within; the fact of the search for Kurtz and for some disclosure concerning him implies that matters of the surface are not enough.

Previously I have suggested that Kurtz remains a voice for Marlow, even after Marlow has confronted him at the Inner Station, and that upon Kurtz's death Marlow exhibits his uncertainty as to whether there was ever anything else to the man but a voice, admitting only that the pilgrims buried "something." This attitude toward Kurtz—and it is never modified—implies a failure by Marlow, for although he struggles into the heart of darkness, declares his sympathetic allegiance to Kurtz, watches the man die, and journeys out again, he ends where he began. Marlow remarks the futility of his position more than once: "...arguing with myself whether or no I would talk openly with Kurtz; but before I could come to any conclusion it occurred to be that my speech or my silence, indeed any action of mine, would be a mere futility.... The essentials of this affair lay deep under the surface, beyond my reach, and beyond my power of meddling" (100).[2]

Marlow's conception of the reality of the wilderness remains as bemused as his idea of the meaning of Kurtz's

[2]Marlow's inadequacy becomes even more emphatic when we consider that here his particular concern appears to be the politics of the trading company, a matter of relative simplicity when compared to his later difficulties with Kurtz.

experience. Although he constantly suggests that at the center of the wilderness lies "the amazing reality of its concealed life" (80), and although he often asserts that he is penetrating "deeper and deeper into the heart of darkness" (95), in his insistence upon the vague and the paradoxical the "purpose" of the wilderness remains always "inscrutable." It escapes definition except in terms of its awesome, vague, and passive magnitude: "...the silent wilderness surrounding this cleared speck on the earth struck me as something great and invincible, like evil or truth" (76). Marlow is no nearer a central reality at the geographical heart of the darkness than he was when, proceeding down the coast, he was aware of a "general sense of vague and oppressive wonder" (62).

It thus seems generally impossible to move beyond the surface in any meaningful way. Reality in this story exists not in the positive but in the negative, for it is all that human disciplines cannot reach, all that lies beyond these disciplines within the center of a man, of a wilderness, and, as Marlow implies, of experience itself. Language too, as all resources of the human imagination, fails in attempting to discover the meaning of Kurtz and of experience: "He was just a word for me. I did not see the man in the name any more than you do. Do you see him? Do you see the story? Do you see anything?...No, it is impossible; it is impossible to convey the life-sensation of any given epoch of one's existence—that which makes its truth, its meaning—its subtle and penetrating essence. It is impossible. We live, as we dream—alone..." (82). Kurtz was a word and remained a word, even when he and Marlow were face to face: attempts to discover a meaning beyond the word failed. And Marlow is not speaking only of Kurtz. He begins with his inability to convey some meaning in terms of Kurtz in Africa, but he continues, characteristically, with the insistence that this inability is universal, that by focusing on Kurtz's particular "aloneness" or remoteness from the world of language there is revealed a general condition of human experience.

Language has meaning, in "Heart of Darkness," in relation to the exteriors of experience—the coast of a wilderness, the surface of a river, a man's appearance and his voice—and this meaning can exist as a reality so long as one remains ignorant, deliberately or otherwise, of all that lies beyond these exteriors, of what language cannot penetrate. For with the intimation that there is something beyond the verbal and, indeed, the imaginative capacities comes the realization that language is insufficient. And if we desire to discover a reality greater than that of words, we are confronted not with the truth within, but with the real disparity between the gimmickry of the human mind and this truth. Because Marlow wishes to know more than surfaces, the reality of surfaces is destroyed. His knowledge of reality may now exist only as his knowledge of the unbridgeable separation between the world of man's disciplined imagination and that something or nothing to which this world is assumed to relate.

Thus whereas Marlow uses the term "reality" in two ways, the reality that he—and a reader—discovers is of a third sort. It is a reality that exists in the realization that "surface" and "heart" are inevitably separate matters and that mind can have ordered awareness only of the former. Marlow's final reality is a state of suspension between the disciplined world of mind and language and the world of essences at the center of experience—whatever these may be—which mind attempts to apprehend but cannot, a dream-state of suggestions and futilities. Marlow is finally aware of both sorts of "reality," certain of neither.

It is for these reasons that Marlow does not view Kurtz's last utterance only as a cry of selfish despair, but declares that Kurtz had "summed up." And as a summation of the imaginative experience of "Heart of Darkness," "the horror!" can have but one meaning: all hearts are in darkness; the morality and meaning with which man surrounds himself and his experience is unreal; the reality of experience lies beyond language and the processes of the human imagination.[3] In revealing this knowledge to Marlow, Kurtz has taken a step that Marlow would not take explicitly: "...he had made that last stride, he had stepped over the edge, while I had been permitted to draw back my hesitating foot" (151). Because he has relinquished his hold upon his ideals and his eloquence, because he has wholly detached himself from matters of the surface, Kurtz is able at last to define, as Marlow sees it, that about which Marlow himself—in his preoccupation with both the reality of the surface and the reality of the "heart"—has been so reluctant and so ambiguous. Marlow is torn,

[3]What Kurtz actually sees, of course, cannot be known, but in relating his vision to the rest of the story we must place it in the scheme of meaning which Marlow has constructed for it. Here it has meaning in the way that I have suggested, although we may well be uncertain regarding Marlow's reliability. This uncertainty is of such proportions, however, that we must ignore its larger implications, for if we do not then "Heart of Darkness" becomes a psychological case history of Marlow's prejudicial concerns and distorted perceptions, and there is, I think, little point or consistency in such an assessment of the story. Even in ignoring these implications, our uncertainty in accepting Marlow's remarks remains a powerful factor in relation to the schematic separation between mind and "reality" that I have discussed. We can never be sure whether Marlow is right about Kurtz's experience, or if Marlow *could* be right.

throughout the story, between the desire to achieve a realization as final as Kurtz's and the conviction that he must deny such a realization if his life is to have any meaning. Kurtz is destroyed in his movement toward and final confrontation of what Marlow views as the ultimate truth: that the essentials of experience remain amoral and, even, alinguistic.

"Heart of Darkness," then, as the account of a journey into the center of things—of Africa, of Kurtz, of Marlow, and of human existence—poses itself as the refutation of such a journey and as the refutation of the general metaphorical conception that meaning may be found within, beneath, at the center. At the end of the search we encounter a darkness, and it is no more defined than at the beginning of the journey and the narrative; it continues to exist only as something unapproachable. The stages of such a journey and such a discourse, the struggle with vagueness and paradox, accompanied always with the feeling that one is not yet at the heart of the matter, must suffice. Once again amid the disciplines and meanings of civilization that are so easily and carelessly assumed to be real, Marlow calls to mind his experience beyond these meanings and declares that anxious ministrations to his weakened body are beside the point: ". . . it was my imagination that wanted soothing" (152).

Most of the parallels between *Moby-Dick* and "Heart of Darkness" should be obvious, but it is perhaps worth-while to remark those that are most important. The pseudo-moralities of the minor characters, for example, as well as the superficial realities of Marlow's and Kurtz's moral and verbal facility, are analogous in their function to the various special languages that Ishmael employs; they seem to demonstrate the existence of something beyond themselves, although at last it becomes apparent that this "something" must simply be defined as unperceivable. But the most important languages of "Heart of Darkness" are those of Marlow and Kurtz. The latter's verbal flexibility is defined as arbitrary and artificial—removed from any intensive relevance to reality by its easy multiplicity. And Marlow's language, like Ishmael's, most often takes the form of statements about language, and I am not speaking only of his self-conscious and explicit descriptions of his own rhetorical method. For Marlow's own "whiteness"—while it is implied in the qualified and complex verbal gestures of his entire narrative—is dramatized, in part, as the voice and the name of Kurtz. If Ishmael, in attempting to perceive, can speak only of his own method and manner of perception, Marlow can describe only Kurtz's voice and its multiple implications, with the recognition that such a procedure must fail to approach the supposed essentials. What is anonymous about Kurtz, in this way, is paradoxically most important and—because it cannot be apprehended—both nonsignificant and insignificant. Marlow both cannot and must believe in the realities of words.

These and other parallels, however, are not as important as the divergences of "Heart of Darkness" from *Moby-Dick*, and it is the development of the fundamental imaginative problem from the one work to the other that I shall now consider. We have seen Melville's preoccupation with the idea of a split universe, with two distinct kinds of reality; we have seen also that for much of the book Ahab stands for the attempt to make the artificial the real, for the imaginative act of penetrating from one to the other, and for the general attitude that meaning may be found "within." The metaphor of attempted penetration is clearly the structural basis of "Heart of Darkness"; Marlow's spatial movement along a coast, up a river, and toward the supposed center of things, although as ultimately inconclusive as Ishmael's course, arouses the sort of expectation that we have associated with Ahab: it seems evidence of a thematic assumption that something beyond surfaces can be apprehended. The fact that Marlow resembles both Ishmael and Ahab is important; it suggests that, as I shall now try to show more conclusively, the polarities of *Moby-Dick* begin to merge in "Heart of Darkness."

In a manner similar to Ahab's insistence upon the reality of something behind the "mask," Marlow constantly asserts the presence of a reality beyond the superficial concerns of work and of all civilized disciplines. Marlow's attitude toward this reality, however, is ambivalent. His imagination, in the first place, is above all a moral imagination, and he declares that the discovery of the reality will destroy the moral meaning of his world; for these reasons he continually suggests that there is something evil about the reality and that one must count himself lucky not to perceive it. Marlow constructs a metaphorical relation similar to Ahab's attitude toward the white whale, and he calls the reality a "darkness." Both Marlow and Ahab usually assert, then, that the ineffable is evil, but Marlow's conception is even more vague and more inclined toward simple negation than Ahab's. In a similar manner, the "darkness" is all around Marlow— it is all that lies within and beyond the details of his experience—whereas for Ahab the unapproachable is concentrated in the white whale. Whatever lies beyond language, in short, has become even less defined, more blurred in its outlines, although Marlow nonetheless insists that it is there.

As we come to understand the problem of "Heart of Darkness," however, we realize that this moral "darknesss" that Marlow posits is finally significant not as a force of evil that is responsible for all human failure, but more simply as an emptiness, the result of an emphatic inability to render experience meaningful in any terms.[4] The vision of reality from which Marlow shrinks is finally suggested to be simply his awareness of defeat, of his failure to go beneath the "surface." And it is the obvious artificiality of surfaces—which include the moral concerns that are so important to him—that is the "darkness." The best specific example of this connection between darkness and emptiness, or perhaps the partial redefinition of darkness as emptiness, is Kurtz's death:

It was as though a veil had been rent. I saw on that ivory face the expression of sombre pride, of ruthless power, of craven terror—of an intense and hopeless despair. Did he live his life again in every detail of desire, temptation, and surrender during that supreme moment of complete knowledge? He cried in a whisper at some image, at some vision. (149)

The uncertainty of *"as though* a veil had been rent" characterizes this moment; Kurtz has a vision that is both remarkable and vague. Marlow suggests here that Kurtz is actually seeing something—and in this way Kurtz resembles Ahab—but in terms of the patterns of images that pervade "Heart of Darkness," as well as of the specifically hesitant, paradoxical, and interrogative quality of the language of this particular passage, Kurtz is crying out that he

---

[4]Compare Albert J. Guerard: "Perhaps the chief contradiction of 'Heart of Darkness' is that it suggests and dramatizes evil as active energy (Kurtz and his unspeakable lusts) but defines evil as vacancy." *Conrad the Novelist* (Cambridge [Mass.]: Harvard University Press, 1958), p. 37.

cannot see. If we are to judge by Kurtz's characteristic emptiness and Marlow's futility, "the horror" is that there is nothing to see.

It should be remembered at this point that the metaphorical attitude that Ahab represents—the antithesis of Ishmael's reliance upon the suggestive artificiality of the similitude—is transformed at the end of *Moby-Dick* into a corroboration of Ishmael's position. Ahab's death not only seems to deny that the ineffable can be perceived but also casts doubt upon whether it exists. Both the nature of the white whale as an incarnation of a supposed reality and the very existence of this reality itself are questioned.

But "Heart of Darkness" goes beyond *Moby-Dick*, for the suggestion that the ineffable may simply be an emptiness is present throughout the story. It is always the hollowness of Kurtz that is important. The darkness is "barren": "Kurtz discoursed. A voice! a voice! It rang deep to the very last. It survived his strength to hide in the magnificent folds of eloquence the barren darkness of his heart" (147). As I have remarked, the barrenness of the "darkness" is indicated also by the futility of Marlow's attempts to establish the reality that lies beyond surfaces, and Kurtz's insight—the "last stride" that Marlow did not take—is in this way suggested to be simply an explicit declaration of the emptiness that Marlow cannot unequivocally admit to be the permanent condition of experience.

I do not mean to imply, however, that the redefinition of "darkness" as nothingness is ever accomplished for Marlow; we must remember that, as he says, he drew back his "hesitating foot," and because he did he is able to take refuge in the idea of a "darkness," the idea of powers beyond the imagination responsible for the defeat of imagination. To Marlow's moral sensibility such an idea is essential; he must have a meaning, even if he himself suspects its artificiality. It is important, too, to note that Marlow declares that his failure to define the matter—to admit finally to a universal barrenness—was only a case of circumstances, of situations in which he was simply insensible. The ambiguity that arises from these fortuitous circumstances is never resolved.

Even though Marlow's characteristic gesture is one that reveals a failure, his moral demands transform this failure into a vague metaphor: the fact that meaning is negated becomes for him the meaning, the "darkness." In this way, I think, a reader may feel that Marlow is being dramatized; he becomes aware of a mind beyond Marlow's, a mind that is intent upon scrutinizing Marlow and his most questionable imaginative act—that of ascribing power to what seems to be nothingness.

The "darkness" itself is thus only a possibility that is shown to be suspect, like Marlow's "evil" or "truth," and even the second assertion of the title of this story—that the "heart" is composed of "darkness"—appears inaccurate. We do not proceed through the known or partially known to the unknown in "Heart of Darkness"; we do not, in fact, proceed at all. The very metaphor upon which the story is constructed—that of penetration to the meaning within— is questioned much more thoroughly than in *Moby-Dick*, so much so that it appears to be simply another superficial artifice of imagination.

By means of recognizing his verbal and moral facility— the same facility that Ishmael displays—as a fiction, Kurtz comes to rend the "veil"; his act, for Marlow, is a penetration, but what is perceived by this act is suggested to be nothing at all. Kurtz begins as an Ishmael and ends as an Ahab, since for both Kurtz and Ahab the final vision serves to cast doubt upon the possibility of vision itself. Like Ahab, Kurtz is finally linked to the kind of unresolved profundity that Ishmael represents. Marlow's own "profundity," of course, resembles Ishmael's, although Marlow seems to have much more at stake. Yet he is also the counterpart of Ahab in his attempts to define Kurtz's experience and the "darkness" unambiguously, and in the fact that these attempts are finally frustrated.[5]

The confusion here is representative, for the separability and the sense of the characteristics of Ishmael and Ahab appear to depend upon the possibility of a reality at the "heart." When a story demonstrates that such a reality can only be significant, in terms of the imagination, as a nothingness, and so persistently denies that the metaphorical connection between an artificial order and a reality beyond the artificial can be made, then the significant characters are left, like Marlow, with suggestive and futile approximations that imply both meaning and meaninglessness: each character, no matter his intentions, is finally an Ishmael.

[5]And Marlow's preservation from Ahab-like destruction, of course, depends not upon the kind of language he uses but only upon his refusal to recognize what this language implies, a refusal facilitated by circumstance.

CHAPTER IV

Absalom, Absalom!
The Extended Simile

ABSALOM, ABSALOM! at first seems to be merely a puzzle. If, as is likely, we assume that novels are usually coherent and consistent, then the incapacities of the narrators who present the first and second accounts of Thomas Sutpen will appear to be temporary difficulties that will at last be solved. The confusing introduction to the story of Sutpen through Mr. Compson and Rosa Coldfield will be followed, we might suppose, by a more able narrator and by relative clarity and comprehension. We find, however, that the third of the principal narrators of the book, Quentin Compson, provides no simplification of the complexities we have encountered. Some of the supposed "facts" have been changed, to be sure, and Sutpen's experiences now appear to make better sense as a sequence of cause and effect. But the circumstances in which this last story is told, Quentin's drastically ambivalent attitude toward the value of his own remarks and perceptions, his relation to his account as it is described by the anonymous narrator, and the implications of that account all suggest that the inability of the narrators to understand the experience surrounding Sutpen may be an expression of a consistent theme: that human experience cannot be understood, that order cannot be created.

The view of the story presented by Quentin's father depends both upon a lack of information—or what a reader assumes, at this point, to be information—and upon the apparent demands of Mr. Compson's own sensibility. In his hands the story becomes not what happened but what, in the absence of certainty as to the facts, he would like to think happened. His narrative is constantly shown to be his own hypothesis as to what "must have been" and is always explicitly bounded by what he is able to imagine and what he prefers to believe.

Mr. Compson's remarks express a great many motives and actions that he cannot explain. And what he cannot explain he characteristically redefines as what cannot be explained and then as evidence of something he calls "chance." In attempting to understand Sutpen's investigation of Bon, he remarks, "You would almost believe that Sutpen's trip to New Orleans was just sheer chance, just a little more of the illogical machinations of a fatality."[1] As may be noted here, "chance" and "fatality" are closely associated, perhaps synonymous, in Mr. Compson's mind and in his story. The movement toward an insistence upon the operation of this chance-fatality is clearly exemplified in the following passage:

...we see dimly people...possessing now heroic proportions, performing their acts of simple passion and simple violence, impervious to time and inexplicable—Yes, Judith, Bon, Henry,

[1]William Faulkner, *Absalom, Absalom!* (New York: Random House, Inc., 1951), p. 102. All subsequent references to *Absalom, Absalom!* are to this edition.

Sutpen: all of them. They are there, yet something is missing; they are like a chemical formula exhumed along with the letters from that forgotten chest...you bring them together in the proportions called for, but nothing happens; you re-read, tedious and intent, poring, making sure that you have forgotten nothing, made no miscalculation; you bring them together again and again nothing happens: just the words, the symbols, the shapes themselves, shadowy inscrutable and serene, against that turgid background of a horrible and bloody mischancing of human affairs. (101)

All of Mr. Compson's important attitudes are present here: his inability to understand the story or even to appreciate the reality of the characters; his concomitant sense of the story as "mischancing"; and an assumption that seems to underlie it all—that these characters possessed "heroic proportions." It appears that Mr. Compson's insistence upon the presence of the inexplicable in his narrative has a partial source in his desire to view the Sutpens as heroes, that by presenting them in conflict with a "fatality" he is able to lend them great stature. In this way, what he cannot explain becomes sacred to him, and "they don't explain" becomes "we are not supposed to know" (100). It is as if he is aware that his view of the story as heroic tragedy depends upon its remaining unexplained and that he is therefore reluctant to pursue his inquiries.

Mr. Compson's heroic view, in fact, is unquestionably self-conscious: "Fate," he suggests, is the "stage manager" (73), and the history of the Sutpens is like a "Greek tragedy" (62). On the one hand, this explicit labeling of his perspective draws our attention to the inadequacy of the view itself, but on the other hand it is evidence of Mr. Compson's own awareness that his understanding of the story arises from a stock metaphor—the world as heroic stage—founded upon what he cannot explain. It may be, in short, that Mr. Compson himself, as well as a reader, is aware that his heroic past is as fictional as Greek tragedy itself. His assertion of such a past will thus seem the result not of a private compulsion but of a more balanced attempt to deal with a circumstantial lack of knowledge and vision.

Because of these limitations that are perhaps psychological and certainly circumstantial, a reader is acutely conscious of the artificiality of Mr. Compson's narrative. This same artificiality, however, seems evidence of a reality to come; Mr. Compson's failure, we suppose, is simply preparation for a speaker of greater imaginative flexibility and fuller knowledge. We imagine that *a* story about Thomas Sutpen will be told—some yet unrevealed story for which Mr. Compson's narrative is a momentary disguise and substitute.

But this more capable speaker is not Rosa Coldfield, for she, like her predecessor, may be seen to transform an inadequacy into a suspect virtue. Rosa continually reveals her feelings of amazement and her inability to make any sense whatever of the story, but at the same time she exhibits a fanatical certainty about it. As in the case of Mr. Compson, the certainty depends upon the inability, for by viewing Sutpen's story as inexplicable in terms of what she judges to be predictable human activity, she is able to insist that the man is superhuman. Sutpen becomes a "demon" who appears out of nowhere to enact an evil fatality:

I saw Judith's marriage forbidden without rhyme or reason or shadow of excuse; I saw Ellen die with only me, a child, to turn to and ask to protect her remaining child; I saw Henry repudiate his home and birthright and then return and practically fling the bloody corpse of his sister's sweetheart at the hem of her wedding gown; I saw that man return—the evil's source and head which had outlasted all its victims—who had created two children not only to destroy one another and his own line, but my line as well, yet I agreed to marry him. (18)

Throughout her narrative Rosa insists that she was a passive observer and the victim of an outrageous fatality beyond her understanding. In the intensity of her failure to understand she declares that the story cannot be understood; she insists further that what is incomprehensible to her must be supernatural.

Rosa's understanding of the story, in other words, is inseparable from her feeling of outrage. She occasionally asserts that Sutpen's goal was "respectability" (16), and at another moment, she is sure that he is driven by "ruthless pride" and a "lust for vain magnificence" (162). These characterizations of Sutpen may be seen to depend upon Rosa's more personal concerns, upon her response to what may have been a proposal of a trial copulation. They depend upon her view of herself as the image of that respectability which Sutpen, in her terms, constantly offended and finally outraged.

It now becomes possible, once again, to see Rosa's narrative as we have seen Mr. Compson's: the narrative problem appears to be a defined psychological problem. But also like Mr. Compson, Rosa Coldfield's supposed psychological difficulties are questioned by her own awareness of the way in which they work; she insists, in fact, upon the fallibility of her perspective: *"there is no such thing as memory: the brain recalls just what the muscles grope for: no more, no less: and its resultant sum is usually incorrect and false and worthy only of the name of dream"* (143). If we say that she sees what she wants to see, we must also admit that she knows that she is doing so.

The problem of perception, however, extends beyond the matter of memory, for Rosa often declares that the very past in which she lived and of which she speaks did not exist for her at the time. This feeling reaches its culmination when she describes Charles Bon, who is to her the most important figure of that past. She loved Bon, she says, with a love founded upon contradiction and paradox, *"beyond the compass of glib books: that love which gives up what it never had"* (149). She loved, as she remarks, a man who may not have ever existed at all except as her own imagined creation, a man she never saw alive or dead: *"That was all. Or rather, not all, since there is no all, no finish.... You see, I never saw him. I never even saw him dead. I heard an echo, but not the shot; I saw a closed door but did not enter it"* (150). What for her is the climax of the story that began with Thomas Sutpen's arrival in Jefferson is exactly that which is most anticlimactic, and what is most important to her is least real. And this was because, she tells us elsewhere, she was then *"living in that womb-like corridor where the world came not even as living echo but as dead incomprehensible shadow"* (162). Bon was unreal to her simply because he was somewhere outside that "corridor," beyond which even the commonplace might have been unreal.

Again as with Quentin's father, Rosa's self-awareness tends to modify a reader's conception of her limitations. If these limitations themselves make us aware of the fictional quality of her narrative, her confession of them suggests that her problem is not largely "psychological" nor even definitely emotional. This feeling is corroborated later when we learn that her sense of outrage and amazement has a more significant source than the insulting of her virginal and respectable self-conception; *"for almost fifty years"* Rosa has asked of Sutpen's second proposal, *"Why?*

Why? and Why?" (167). Whereas before her inability to comprehend the experience of which she tells seemed to be the product of a lesser, simply old-maidish outrage, at this point her failure appears the result of a genuine, even desperate attempt to understand.

In both the case of Mr. Compson and that of Rosa, then, internal, psychological difficulties seem less important than the sheer external facts of their situations. Rosa's awareness of her failure deflects the emphasis from a supposed neurosis within her to something acting upon her from without—a "corridor," a set of limitations which she somehow cannot escape. The emphasis upon circumstances in her case, it appears, is even greater than for Mr. Compson.

A reader may assume even now, however, that *Absalom, Absalom!* is a novel like other novels, that a story exists and will be told. No matter how circumstantial the narrative insufficiencies of Quentin's father and Rosa Coldfield may seem, as insufficiencies they are inseparable from the characters themselves, and we continue to expect a better speaker; the narrative difficulties, we suppose, are still difficulties that the last character-narrator of the novel—Quentin Compson—will not have.

Both Rosa and Mr. Compson are present in the story that Quentin tells. While the long, frequently interrupted dialogue with Shreve in a room at Harvard is always subject to his modification and approval, the narrative that it comprises is an amalgamation of the narratives of many: General Compson, Mr. Compson, Rosa, Shreve, and of course Quentin himself.[2] This section of the novel, that is,

[2]Because this "dialogue" is always subject to Quentin's approval, we may for the sake of economy of reference consider it as a unified section of the narrative. In my discussion, also, I rely much more upon Quentin's remarks than upon Shreve's, for the latter may be

contains narrative matter and techniques that we recognize, and both Shreve and Quentin are aware, more specifically, that they sound like "father."

One aspect of Quentin's own particular method, however, is immediately apparent. In the narratives of Rosa and his father it is the limitations of these speakers that are initially most striking and most revealing, but Quentin's story is different. For the first time in the novel a reader is presented with a powerfully imagined narrative that—no matter how much it may be questioned ultimately nor how puzzling its arrangement—is in general consistent and reasonable within itself.

Quentin's relation to the story he tells is often characterized as that of direct perception: "It seemed to Quentin that he could actually see" (132). This remark is on occasions simply repeated verbatim, on others slightly modified. And at times it serves to introduce a narrative of startling imaginative intensity, as, for example, when Henry Sutpen and Bon confront each other on an approach to Sutpen's Hundred, one brother about to destroy the other. Considering that Quentin is frequently described as a seer, that he has moments of clarity that other narrators do not have, and that the story he tells seems to work as a story, he appears to be the narrator we have been awaiting, who will endow the story with meaning and imaginative reality.

It is necessary to notice, however, that it only *seems* to Quentin that he can see. The limitation that begins here in the word "seems" grows larger when we consider that Quentin is often described as exhibiting a quality that is

_____

the only unquestionable psychopathological case in the novel—in his capacity for sadism, the emphatic vicariousness of his pleasures, and so on.

generally antithetical to his supposed imaginative vitality.
He is said to speak in a "flat, curiously dead voice" (258),
or in an "almost sullen flat tone" (255); he displays a
"brooding bemusement" in a room that is "tomb-like."
Quentin also reveals explicitly his feeling of tiredness, of
repetition, and of deadness, and what is most interesting
about these revelations is their contrast with his imaginative powers. This paradox, of course, has a literary prece-
dent; it might simply be the stock schizophrenia of the
seer, the man whose powers of vision are extraordinary but
who is exhausted by them because he, at last, is only mortal.
In Quentin's case, however, the paradox stems not from
an emphasis upon his imaginative activity, but from an
insistence upon his passivity: *"Yes,"* he thinks, *"I have
heard too much, I have been told too much; I have had to
listen to too much"* (207). This paradox of vitality and
deadness, of Quentin as active seer and passive sounding
board for all the voices he has ever heard, is pervasive in
his narrative, and, considering our optimistic view of his
perspective, this paradox is crucial.

Quentin's exhausted despair is most often associated with
the voice of his father, and it is suggested in this way that
Quentin's problem may be, as in the possible views of
previous narrators, psychological. But this obsessive concern with his father is only significant and, perhaps, only
exists for him in terms of the telling of the story:

Am I going to have to have to hear it all again he thought *I am
going to have to hear it all over again I am already hearing it
all over again I am listening to it all over again I shall have to
never listen to anything else but this again forever so apparently not only a man never outlives his father but not even
his friends and acquaintances do.* (277)

This paradox of imaginative vitality as opposed to exhaustion and deadness is aligned with another, which comes to our attention when Quentin tells Shreve that it was he, Quentin, who told his father the rest of the story on the basis of what he discovered out at Sutpen's mansion, and when he admits that at the mansion, even though he saw Clytie and Henry Sutpen, he was told nothing. Shreve says: ". . . it just came out of the terror and the fear after she turned you loose. . . and she looked at you and you saw it was not rage but terror. . . and she didn't tell you in the actual words because even in the terror she kept the secret; nevertheless she told you, or at least all of a sudden you knew—" (350–351). The case for Quentin's clairvoyance that Shreve presents here may be seen to be a substantiation of the vitality I have mentioned, and a reader may feel that Quentin really can know without being told, and see without knowing. In view of the narrators that have preceded him, however, and of our awareness of his own sense of frustration and futility, the fact that Quentin's vision springs from what is apparently nothing becomes a problem. In his discovery of Henry Sutpen at the mansion we may see an enactment of this polarity of vision and nothingness, and this dramatic moment itself, I think, takes the form of a negation of vision and of imaginative vitality. The impact of the supposed dialogue between Quentin and Henry is great, but this impact depends upon the fact that nothing is said:

And you are——?
Henry Sutpen.
And you have been here——?
Four years.
And you came home——?
To die. Yes.

78

Absalom, Absalom!

To die?
Yes. To die.
And you have been here——?
Four years.
And you are——?
Henry Sutpen. (373)

This dialogue is a kind of play within a play; it is a crystallization of the sources of Quentin's vision and of the vision itself: nothing happens and nothing is said, but Quentin sees and knows. The qualities of this moment, of course, are anything but persuasive as to the reality or relevance of Quentin's imaginative perceptions. If his vision arises out of clairvoyance, this very clairvoyance has the tone of despair: in Quentin the moment of supposed perception is dramatized as a moment of hypnotic and futile circularity. This dialogue serves, rather than to demonstrate Quentin's powers as a seer, to reassert the elements of the paradox I have noted: it possesses imaginative intensity and the suggestion of meaning as opposed to its circularity and deadness, and I suggest that the sense of torturous repetition here is the same as that which Quentin feels in his despair at hearing and telling the story again and again. Here, however, we realize that this hypnotic futility lies at the foundation of Quentin's imaginative vitality; his vitality arises from deadness.

There is nothing but the talking, it seems, and the talking is dead, futile, circular. Quentin's narrative is significant not as the resolution that a reader has expected but only as the summation of all the speculation and misguided intensity that has preceded it. The anonymous narrator—whom we may associate with Faulkner—defines the Quentin-Shreve dialogue in these terms: "...the two of them creating between them, out of the rag-tag and bob-ends of old tales and talking, people who perhaps had never existed at all anywhere" (303). Henry Sutpen, we know, "existed," but he existed only as part of a dialogue that is for Quentin the reminder of his failure to understand what the story means, the reminder that each attempt to understand, each vision, arises out of a moment of failure. Quentin's very assertion that he "knows" is inseparable from his conviction that he cannot know—a conviction displayed in his sense of futile repetition, in his implied awareness that his ability to "see" is based upon this same futility, and in a simple, literal admission to Shreve. "Do you understand it?" Shreve asks, and the exchange continues:

"I dont know," Quentin said. "Yes, of course I understand it." They breathed in the darkness. After a moment Quentin said: "I dont know."

"Yes. You dont know. You dont even know about the old dame, the Aunt Rosa."

"Miss Rosa," Quentin said.

"All right. You dont even know about her.... Do you?"

"No," Quentin said peacefully. He could taste the dust. (362)

Quentin resembles his father and Rosa Coldfield in that his story is founded upon what he cannot know, but he is distinguished from them by the persistence and intensity of his attempt to make the story meaningful. There is a distinct progression in *Absalom, Absalom!* from the placid and remote speculation of Mr. Compson through the narrow but more immediate incapacity of Rosa to Quentin's attempt, and this final attempt is both more ambitious and more seriously frustrated than those of previous narrators. It is no longer a question of Mr. Compson's errors or Rosa's ignorance: there can be no errors or ignorance in a narrative world where we are concerned with what cannot be meaningful or what may not exist as comprehensible experience at all.

Instead of an answer to what we had assumed was a puzzle, we encounter in Quentin's narrative the indication that the puzzle itself may not be real, that the gap between experience and meaning in this novel must remain unbridgeable, and that the narrative is only, after all, words, only a product of "old tales and talking." The paradox of Quentin's narrative is that he forms this "talking" into a vital, articulated vision while demonstrating—and of this he is aware—that its basis is only dead speculation upon a dead past.

The tension between imagined reality and empty words that we find sustained in Quentin's narrative is never resolved in *Absalom, Absalom!* It may be said to be explained, however, if we consider its relation to the unreal story it creates, to the conception and progress of Thomas Sutpen's "design."

"Sutpen's trouble was innocence," we are told as Quentin begins his account. "All of a sudden he discovered, not what he wanted to do but what he just had to do, had to do it whether he wanted to or not" (220). Sutpen has been sent with a message to the mansion of a white planter whom he has repeatedly watched lounging in a barrel-stave hammock; he is thinking of the house and "thinking how at last he was going to see the inside of it, see what else a man was bound to own who could have a special nigger to hand him his liquor" (229). A "monkey nigger" meets him at the door, and even while he is talking, telling Sutpen never to come to the front door again, Sutpen has flashes of memory concerning his previous experience with Negroes:

You knew that you could hit them, he told Grandfather, and they would not hit back or even resist. But you did not want to, because they (the niggers) were not it, not what you wanted to hit; that you knew when you hit them you would just be hitting a child's toy balloon with a face painted on it, a face slick and smooth and distended and about to burst into laughing, and so you did not dare strike it because it would merely burst and you would rather let it walk on out of your sight than to have stood there in the loud laughing. (230)

"The niggers" somehow prevent one's assaulting whatever it is that is important; their faces are the faces of balloons that—if one takes action against them—burst into laughter, "the roaring waves of mellow laughter meaningless and terrifying and loud" (232). Sutpen characterizes the barrier that prevents him from entering the house as something so artificial and empty as to be unassailable, a barrier that can only serve to reassert the futility of his situation.

The parallels between Sutpen and Ahab here are so striking as to be worth detailed comment. The significance of the "monkey nigger" for Sutpen is that of an artificial barrier that prevents him from penetrating to what he has assumed is a reality. Ahab would call it a "pasteboard mask"; for Sutpen it is a "balloon face." Ahab, on the one hand, is conscious of many such masks in the visual and verbal universe; they are all the suggestions, omens, and half-meanings that torture him in their uncertainty and multiplicity. Sutpen's particular problem at the moment, on the other hand, is less sophisticated and more simply a matter of deprivation. It is a social, not a natural, artificiality with which he is concerned, and this single absence of meaning —the fact that he cannot enter the house—becomes for him, as I shall try to show later, a universal negation. The color significance works almost too well here: Ahab's tortured uncertainty is incarnated in the "colorless all-color" of whiteness, whereas Sutpen's sense of complete futility and negation is symbolized in the blackness of the "monkey nigger." Both colors are generally significant as the expressions of a nothingness.

Sutpen is not yet, however, explicitly conscious of such a nothingness. He runs into the woods and attempts to understand what has happened. It was not the "nigger" that was important, he later tells General Compson:

The nigger was just another balloon face slick and distended ...during that instant in which, before he knew it, something in him had escaped and—he unable to close the eyes of it—was looking out from within the balloon face just as the man who did not even have to wear the shoes he owned, whom the laughter which the balloon held barricaded and protected from such as he, looked out from whatever invisible place he (the man) happened to be at the moment, at the boy outside the barred door in his patched garments and splayed bare feet, looking through and beyond the boy, he himself seeing his own father and sisters and brothers as the owner, the rich man (not the nigger) must have been seeing them all the time—as cattle, creatures heavy and without grace, brutely evacuated into a world without hope or purpose for them, who would in turn spawn with brutish and vicious prolixity, populate, double treble and compound...with for sole heritage that expression on a balloon face bursting with laughter which had looked out at some unremembered and nameless progenitor who had knocked at a door when he was a little boy and had been told by a nigger to go around to the back. (234–235)

What Sutpen himself appears to mean by the discovery of his "innocence" is the birth of a kind of self-consciousness; "something in him had escaped," and as the white owner has done before and does now Sutpen looks out upon himself. In terms of this view Sutpen and his descendants become purposeless animals, participants in a brutish chaos whose heritage is the balloon face and the laughter.

The boy's feelings of senselessness and futility are defined in terms of the plantation owner's position inside the big white house. He reflects that he can do nothing to reach the man, that if the house were on fire he would be unable to warn its owner:

> ...*there aint any good or harm either in the living world that I can do to him.* It was like that, he said, like an explosion— a bright glare that vanished and left nothing, no ashes nor refuse; just a limitless flat plain with the severe shape of his intact innocence rising from it like a monument; that innocence instructing him as calm as the others had ever spoken, using his own rifle analogy to do it with, and when it said *them* in place of *he* or *him,* it meant more than all the human puny mortals under the sun that might lie in hammocks all afternoon with their shoes off: He thought 'If you were fixing to combat them that had the fine rifles, the first thing you would do would be to get yourself the nearest thing to a fine rifle you could borrow or steal or make, wouldn't it?' and he said Yes. (238)

Sutpen feels a complete impotence; his significance is totally negative. The awareness of negation, which was previously suggested in blackness, now takes a spatial form. He conceives an image of himself rising from a "plain" that is flat and without limits, and his "innocence" is defined both as this image in the midst of nothingness and that which instructs him how to overcome the nothingness. He must combat "them," and "them" means more, we are told, than a group of socially defined mortals; it is not simply the class, perhaps, but the rules by which the class is established. He will combat these rules by means of the possessions that express the rules, by means of the signs and tokens of the social system, "land and niggers and a fine house" (238).

Sutpen's design is thus social in form; he is attempting to make use of the social system to overcome that system. Like Ahab, he attacks the artificial quality of his experience—which separates him from what he assumes will be a reality—and like Ahab Sutpen employs as a means of progress the artificial itself, the social structure that prevents him from entering the house. By entering the house, Sutpen will be enabled to transform himself and his descendants. They are to be "riven forever free from brutehood" and to have—like Sutpen himself—a meaningful identity (261).

This identity is finally based on the acquiring of possessions, which in accordance with the social structure will express the meaning that Sutpen desires. In Ahab's case a multiple artifice is to be penetrated and reduced to a single revelation by one final thrust of a harpoon; for Sutpen the void of his life is to be filled with possessions and descendants, which in turn must be expressive of a completely controlled and defined design. What the meaning of the design is, exactly, has not been defined as yet; Sutpen, in fact, does not seem to know what it is, but he is convinced that it will be meaning, an alleviation of his vision of chaos and impotence.

A reader's conception of the nature of Sutpen's design takes its form at the outset from what seems antithetical to the design—hollowness, arbitrariness, unreality, impotence —and this continues to be so as he proceeds through the story of Sutpen. For example, Sutpen's first wife, as we learn from the speculations of Quentin and Shreve, was part Negro; it is this that Sutpen appears to be talking about when he declares that a certain aspect of his wife and child would have made his work toward the design an "ironic delusion," and he later enlarges upon this as follows: "I was faced with condoning a fact which had been foisted upon me without my knowledge during the process of building toward my design, which meant the absolute and irrevocable negation of the design; or in holding to my original plan for the design in pursuit of which I had incurred this negation" (273).[3] This passage is characteristic of those by which Sutpen and the narrators express the design; in it there is defined a particular negation of the design, a specific and temporary failure, and the design is given shape in terms of what it is not.

It is the Negro blood in his wife and son, we may suppose, to which Sutpen objects and that constitutes this particular "negation," and it seems clear that the design is intensely social in its method. It is just the fanatical intensity of Sutpen's supposedly social aspirations, in fact, that is most problematic. Quentin remarks that Sutpen need not have rejected his wife and child, that he might have bluffed the matter out somehow, but that he was apparently forced to reject them by his "conscience" (266). The quality of this "conscience" may be illuminated if we consider Sutpen's later refusal to recognize the same child, now Charles Bon, as his son—the refusal that ultimately results in the collapse of the entire design.

Bon's visits to the plantation, as Mr. Compson suggests to Quentin, are a metaphorical re-enactment of Sutpen's childhood experience: ". . . he stood there at his own door, just as he had imagined, planned, designed, and sure enough after fifty years the forlorn nameless and homeless lost child came to knock at it and no monkey-dressed nigger anywhere under the sun to come to the door and order the

[3]This sentence may be best understood if we observe a grammatical parallelism that Faulkner has neglected to establish: read "or *with* holding" for "or *in* holding."

child away" (267). No "monkey-dressed nigger," perhaps, because now the boy himself, Bon, contains in his Negro blood the means of his own prohibition; in this way Sutpen need not order him away; at any rate, he does not. He simply does nothing. He refuses to take the only action that would alleviate the problem and enable him to continue with his design; he refuses to recognize Bon on any terms. It is as if his childhood imaginings have come true: a boy comes to tell a man that his house is on fire and cannot be heard.[4]

Sutpen has declared to General Compson, we are told, that he felt he had made a mistake somewhere and that his inaction toward Bon—"the fact that for a time he did nothing and so perhaps helped to bring about the very situation which he dreaded"—was "not the result of any failing of courage or shrewdness or ruthlessness, but. . .the result of his conviction that it had all come from a mistake and until he discovered what that mistake had been he did not intend to risk making another one" (268). The language of this passage is mild considering the duration and the intensity of Sutpen's paralysis; his refusal to recognize Bon in any way seems insane, out of all proportion to what we suppose are the facts, and out of proportion even to the sustained bemusement that Sutpen is said to have ad-

[4]The phenomenon of impotence is thus dramatized also in the hypothetical account of Bon, a search for design in itself. Richard Poirier has remarked that "incest with Judith or death at the hands of his brother become the only ways in which Bon can identify himself as Sutpen's son." "Strange Gods in Jefferson, Mississippi," in *William Faulkner: Two Decades of Criticism*, ed. Frederick J. Hoffman and Olga W. Vickery (East Lansing: Michigan State College Press, 1951), p. 239. For explicit images, in Shreve's account, of Bon's failure to "penetrate" and his encounters with "nothingness," see in *Absalom, Absalom!*, for example, pp. 320, 327, 348.

mitted. The "choice" that he felt he had to make, as we learn later, was no choice at all; either way his design would have been destroyed. But in his choice he made no provision for direct action toward Bon, but only for either playing his "last trump card"—telling Henry that Bon is part Negro—or doing nothing.

What is truly inexplicable here is that Bon seems to pose no literal threat whatever to the design; if exposed as a fractionally Negro son he could not participate in the design or even oppose it, and Sutpen might have known this as well as Bon. If the only important consideration were social, also, Sutpen could have either accepted Bon and concealed his Negro blood or refused to accept him and proclaimed it. In either case a merely social design would have been unimpaired. Because Bon is surely not an insurmountable obstacle to the design in social terms, the failure to recognize him becomes significant evidence that Sutpen's demands are more than social, that if he is making use of the particular ingredients of the social system to accomplish his design, the design itself is to be defined not in terms of that system but of something more. It is more, in short, than the sum of its apparent parts.

Sutpen's frantic inaction toward Bon reveals the two important qualities of his design: that it is both an attempt to dominate the arbitrariness that Sutpen perceives in his universe and an attempt to make real the artificial significances that this arbitrariness creates. Sutpen, perhaps, sees Bon as an incarnation of both the arbitrary and the artificial, as the reincarnation, in fact, of the "monkey nigger" of his childhood and all that that figure represented. We must remember, in this connection, that before his experience at the door of the plantation house Sutpen did not question the chaos of "luck" in which he lived; it was only after that experience that this chaos became significant in terms of the meaning, or lack of meaning, of his life. In that moment at the door, Sutpen begins to demand meaning of his experience; he begins to view his world metaphorically. It is just this metaphorical vision, as I have suggested, that is most apparent when he confronts Charles Bon: Bon's Negro blood is literally insignificant, but for Sutpen it implies a crucial lack of control over past and present; in his metaphorical view it represents the total negation that he experienced at the door of the plantation house, where he first became conscious of a possible world of meaning that was beyond him. The characteristic irony of Sutpen's situation is that his demands for meaning, his fierce attempts to create a metaphor from the arbitrariness of his experience, are frustrated even in their conception; when viewed metaphorically this experience yields only what a reader may see as images that imply the unreality of metaphor—a limitless plain, a blackness, a paralysis.

The relentlessness of Sutpen's insistence upon clarity and control in his experience is constantly revealed in his treatment of what a reader might have assumed to be only literal details. He is not content with merely owning slaves, for which the social system provides, but must on numerous occasions strip to the waist and engage a Negro in savage, hand-to-hand combat, fighting until the Negro can fight no longer. This apparently insane desire to dominate his slaves again dramatizes the connection in Sutpen's mind between literal control over the elements of the system he employs and the metaphorical vision of blackness—of unreal significance and negation of self—that he possesses. By defeating the Negro, Sutpen is not only destroying a social artificiality in the relation of the parts of his design to himself but also destroying what he sees metaphorically to be the continued existence of that negation which his design was to overcome.

His will to dominate, of course, is not always displayed in such direct association to the specific metaphor of blackness, but it is always an indication of his desire for unambiguous meaning. We may consider, for example, his treatment of the French architect who designs his plantation house. He does not simply employ the architect, but possesses him completely until the house is finished. The set of conventions which the architect represents are thus redefined as Sutpen's own conventions—not arbitrary significances from a world outside Sutpen, but a part of his very being.

It should be apparent, then, that to Sutpen's mind the complete possession and control of the previously uncontrolled details of experience must inevitably result in the creation of a meaningful identity, that the clarity which is to follow from this control will be an alleviation of disorder and meaninglessness. The physical and literal order of his design are in this way an imaginative order, and his entire progress toward a moment when all the details will fall into place is an uncompromising imaginative act.

Throughout his life the desire for unambiguous order dominates Sutpen's imagination; at every crucial moment in his progress toward failure he views the details of his world as the ingredients of a metaphorical structure that he believes he can and must create. In a conversation with General Compson, he reveals the most important elements of such a metaphor; he reduces his design to what are for him its most important terms: "You see, all I wanted was just a son. Which seems to me, when I look at my contemporary scene, no exorbitant gift from nature or circumstance to demand—" (292). The very simplicity of this statement renders it incomprehensible as a literal remark, for Sutpen had two sons—two sons whose literal destruction was brought about by his demands for control and meaning, by his metaphorical view in which Charles Bon was the negation of such control.

Sutpen's conception of fatherhood, as his conception of the entire world, is founded upon the conviction that the begetting of a son is not a physical or a literal act, but an imaginative and metaphorical achievement; fatherhood is the creation of the essential element in a design, in a structure that will endure. His only desire in the years of his decline is to beget the evidence of his significance, and by doing so to complete the arrangement that he feels is not yet right; the result is the proposal that outrages Rosa Coldfield and which Quentin's father calls another "failing" of Sutpen's shrewdness. A reader, however, may wonder what else at this point Sutpen could have done, given his assumption that his mistake must lie in the arrangement and details of his design. He was a master of detail, but his mastery only resulted in failure. The futile circularity of his course is crystallized in his attempt to father a son upon Milly Jones, whose situation is reminiscent of Sutpen's own childhood, and whose grandfather bears the same relation to the balloon faces and the laughter of Negroes as did Sutpen himself as a child, but who endures it by means of the delusion that he is Sutpen. To Wash Jones "this world where he walked always in mocking and jeering echoes of nigger laughter, was just a dream and an illusion and . . . the actual world was the one where his own lonely apotheosis (Father said) galloped on the black thoroughbred" (282). Sutpen's desire for a son, in this way, brings him back to his origins, back to the brutish senselessness and lack of significance that the laughter first made apparent and that were to become the motivation of his design. Wash Jones views Sutpen as his (Jones's) apotheosis and later destroys him and it, just as Sutpen himself—in his final equivalence to Wash—has returned to his sources and thereby destroyed the apotheosis of himself that was half-created but could not endure: that apotheosis by which he was both the creator of meaning and the product of his creation, the meaning itself, all opposed to the senseless and absurd condition where at last he ends as he began.

General Compson's remarks often support the view of the "apotheosis" that I am suggesting. He declares that Sutpen's failure must be defined in terms of a tension between sense and senselessness, between a "code" and a "maelstrom of unpredictable and unreasoning human beings" (275). And at moments he indicates that it is a matter of even greater proportions, as in Quentin's secondhand account of Sutpen's overseeing of the West Indian plantation:

And he overseeing it, riding peacefully about on his horse while he learned the language (that meager and fragile thread, Grandfather said, by which the little surface corners and edges of men's secret and solitary lives may be joined for an instant now and then before sinking back into the darkness where the spirit cried for the first time and was not heard and will cry for the last time and will not be heard then either), not knowing that what he rode upon was a volcano, hearing the air tremble and throb at night with the drums and the chanting and not knowing that it was the heart of the earth itself he heard, who believed (Grandfather said) that earth was kind and gentle and that darkness was merely something you saw, or could not see in.... (251)

Here General Compson has constructed a metaphor by

which the incomprehensibilities and confusions of human experience are not particular or momentary difficulties to be resolved by better language, but the expressions of a failure that is absolute and inevitable. The metaphor is that of a "darkness," a darkness that is not "merely something you saw, or could not see in."

But while Quentin's grandfather appears to suggest that the only metaphor that can be created is a vague expression of unavoidable defeat, Sutpen's glimpses of the supposed nothingness only goad him to more violent attempts to overcome it. He cannot understand the perpetuation of his impotence; he assumes again and again that he has made a mistake in the details of his design. We are told that Sutpen never loses his innocence, and this innocence may be finally defined as his conviction that the world consists of potential metaphor that need only be accumulated and arranged in order to be real.

And yet the essential quality and paradox of Sutpen's metaphorical vision of the world, again, is that by means of this vision he perceives nothing but the contradictions of it. His determination to establish order, as I have suggested, springs not only from a perception of disorder but also from a vision in which disorder becomes a void, a nothingness. His imagination, in this way, is constantly at war with itself; his attempt to overcome a lack of control, to accumulate and arrange the details of his design, is always at odds with his feeling that this lack of control is evidence of a complete absence of identity, an absolute negation of the "self" that he is striving to create. Sutpen may thus be seen both to deny and to accept General Compson's awareness of a universal "darkness." In Charles Bon, for example, he sees both a simple, literal "mistake" that might be rectified and an absolute, metaphorical contradiction of his ability to create a meaning that, while he cannot admit it as a complete negation of his efforts, paralyzes him, prevents him from acting upon the "mistake." When we consider General Compson's attitude, we may understand why Sutpen's innocence was associated with nothingness in the very conception of his design, for this innocence is what persuades Sutpen throughout his career that meaning can and must be created from disorder even while he appears to view this same disorder as the evidence of absolute negation.

The course of his design is not simply circular; it is no course at all. His conviction that the world consists of potential metaphor that only needs arranging—the conviction that is the guiding principle of this design and of all design—is inseparable from his sense of perfect futility. His maniacal desire to dominate his world is thus explained, for even a momentary failure becomes the metaphorical expression of the void in which he somehow believes and yet which he cannot accept. His attempt to make his world a metaphor succeeds only in reasserting that the only possible metaphor is that of "darkness."

Sutpen's design thus contains its own destruction, and his course of action and vision is inevitably a series of failures. The particular failures of Sutpen, however, may seem unsatisfactory to a reader as evidence for a more general failure. It is possible to reject General Compson's conviction that all is a darkness, in terms of which, as I have tried to show, the interdependence in Sutpen's design between the desire for meaning and the feeling of ultimate failure is revealed.

The question that arises is whether such a connection between not only order and disorder but also meaning and darkness is necessary throughout the world of this novel, for in Sutpen's case it seems suspect in two ways. The vision of meaninglessness from which the design arises and which it implies throughout in the manner of its failures may be questioned if we consider Sutpen's naïveté—the naïveté of a boy born in the mountains of West Virginia and possessing perhaps the simplest code of logic and morality. If, when this code is destroyed, he becomes aware of the complete absence of meaning, it is possible to say that this awareness is simply a product of the narrowness of his mind. In the same manner, both the intensity and the failure of the man's struggle toward his design, depending as they do upon the initial vision, may be seen as a mania arising from the outrage of a peculiarly rigid imagination. In short, the childhood vision was just what half of Sutpen's mind thought it was: only a temporary confusion that could be, with the right method, alleviated. The second objection, then, is that Sutpen does not use the right method, that there is something wrong with the particular metaphor that he is trying to create. Because the implements of his design are those of the social structure of the South, and because he wields these implements with even more ruthless energy than they permit in the first place, we might conclude that Sutpen is simply an immoral man in a moral book, and that therefore he must fail.

It may be noted that here Sutpen is again the counterpart of Ahab, for we have seen that the latter figure can be viewed in just these terms: as a monomaniac whose limitations are those of insanity and folly or as a being of heroic stature who may be termed insane only because he attempts to move beyond the fatal limits of his world. And to view Sutpen as immoral or even insane, of course, is to reduce his significance drastically. In its relation to the narrative method of Quentin, however, and to the paradox of vitality and deadness that I have mentioned, the history of Sutpen's design becomes meaningful, as I shall now show more clearly, as one expression of the fallibility of all order and all imagination in *Absalom, Absalom!* If Sutpen's problem may be termed a kind of imaginative schizophrenia, his particular insanity is general throughout the entire novel.

I have previously dwelt at length upon Quentin's failure to understand the story he articulates, but it is necessary at this point to examine a few details of this failure in order to show that it correlates with Sutpen's history so as to illuminate the structural theme of the novel. When Quentin admits his lack of comprehension to Shreve, for example, he does so "peacefully," and at that moment he can taste the "dust." The "dust" is the dust rising around the buggy as he and Rosa Coldfield make their nocturnal journey to Sutpen's Hundred:

...the dust cloud moving on, enclosing them with not threat exactly but maybe warning, bland, almost friendly, warning, as if to say, *Come on if you like. But I will get there first; accumulating ahead of you I will arrive first, lifting, sloping gently upward under hooves and wheels so that you will find no destination but will merely abrupt gently onto a plateau and a panorama of harmless and inscrutable night and there will be nothing for you to do but return.* (175)

The dust is suggestive not only of mortality but also of chaos; it is the precursor of a "plateau" that resembles the flat plain of meaninglessness in Sutpen's childhood vision; it implies that when Quentin arrives he will discover *"nothing."*[5] And although Henry Sutpen is there at the

[5]The connection between mortality and disorder in the imagination of Quentin and Faulkner himself becomes most obvious in *The Sound and the Fury,* which I shall consider later.

mansion, Quentin learns nothing from him. His supposed actual conversation with Henry demonstrates that there is indeed nothing to do but return. In this way the flashes of perception that Quentin displays are implied to be parallel to Sutpen's design in that both arise from a precognition of meaninglessness and from a subsequent, anticlimactic awareness of a flat and barren nothingness.

Another parallel to Sutpen arises when the anonymous narrator describes the room at Harvard as "this snug monastic coign, this dreamy and heatless alcove of what we call the best of thought." The room is the point of most advantage, where the history of the Sutpens will certainly be understood if it can be. The narrator continues by remarking that Mr. Compson's letter has filled the room with "unratiocinative djinns and demons" (258). The room is filled, perhaps, with the ghostly presences of the Sutpens, who are "unratiocinative" in some supposed lack of systematic thought. Somewhat later the matter becomes clearer: "in the cold room...dedicated to that best of ratiocination which after all was a good deal like Sutpen's morality and Miss Coldfield's demonizing..." (280). An explicit equivalence is drawn here between the logic of Sutpen that failed and the logic of Quentin and Shreve as they attempt to comprehend the failure; they indulge in the "best of thought" and are able only to demonstrate their own similarity to Sutpen and to the narrators that have preceded them.

Earlier Quentin visualizes the death of Thomas Sutpen in a way that further supports the schematic organization for the novel that I am proposing: "...*she heard the whip too though not the scythe, no whistling air, no blow, nothing since always that which merely consummates punishment evokes a cry while that which evokes the last silence occurs in silence"* (185). Sutpen's death evokes "the last silence," and that silence is the entire narrative of *Absalom, Absalom!* All of the particular uncertainties, inadequacies, and cruxes of this narrative, although they may appear to be of only temporary significance initially, are shown to have a larger relevance; they are all part of a general and absolute inability to render experience meaningful—an inability that the supposed story of Sutpen itself implies.

Sutpen's problem, then, becomes part of a larger, thematic problem. And it must be added here that unlike Quentin's father and Rosa, whose information is incomplete, Sutpen is a master of detail; he accumulates all the literal facts necessary to his design. In his own terms, of course, he is sure that he has made a mistake in detail, but, again, his mistake is shown to be of greater dimensions than this—a mistake of vision itself, that "innocent" vision which dictates that the world is metaphor and must mean something, and in terms of which a disorder becomes a "darkness."

This is the vision to which every narrator in the novel holds in his account of Sutpen. Mr. Compson's attitude that the story does not explain is understandable considering his lack of "information"; his mistake lies in the fact that he sees this inexplicability as a metaphor. The inconsistency of details, for him, is an expression of a great meaning that has to do with fate. Rosa, too, possesses a view of the world as metaphor. Her inability to understand Sutpen and the events surrounding him is significant to her as an expression of Sutpen's demonhood. She seems superior to Quentin's father, however, in the intensity with which she asserts the unreality of the experience upon which the story is founded and in the apparently greater cost of her frustrated attempts to give it meaning. She may be said to question her own metaphors more thoroughly.

In Quentin's case the matter of the story appears to become more consistent; of the narrators of the book he is most analogous to Sutpen in that he too is capable in the accumulation of details, details that should comprise a pattern that will be controlled and significant. Nonetheless he cannot understand, cannot achieve the meaning that both he and Shreve think exists. His inability is partly expressed, again, in his sources, in the approximations that he inherits from Rosa and from his father and grandfather as well as in his perceptions that seem to arise from nothing. His most crucial moment of vision takes place in the dialogue, which is so hypnotically repetitive, with Henry Sutpen. This dialogue indicates that what I have called "approximations" and "nothing" are really in Quentin's case the same thing and the same source. We have been prepared for it as a climactic moment of understanding and as such it is a failure. And it is a failure that repeats itself, the repetition suggesting that it means something, that it is a metaphor, and the same repetition denying that the metaphor can be realized. In this way it is equivalent to all the stories that Quentin has heard since he was old enough to listen, stories repeated over and over, whose unfulfilled reiteration both asserts their metaphorical nature and denies it.

It is this tension between the meaningful and the meaningless that Quentin has inherited in the approximations of his father, and it is understandable that he feels he must escape from his father and hence from the unrealized story itself. His only moment of peace in the novel comes when for a moment he dissolves the tension, relinquishes the need for meaning that was bequeathed to him as a history of uncertainties, and admits to Shreve "peacefully" that he does not understand.[6]

In a remark that is relevant to the idea of the "last silence," the anonymous narrator speaks of Sutpen as "Quentin's Mississippi shade who in life had acted and reacted to the minimum of logic and morality, who dying had escaped it completely, who dead remained not only indifferent but impervious to it, somehow a thousand times more potent and alive" (280). Sutpen is more "alive" because he is impervious to attempts to understand him. The meanings that surround him lend him a vitality that arises out of their impotence and deadness. The analogy with the supposed story of Sutpen himself is clear, for in that story his presence and power depended upon impotence not simply in the motivation but in the definition of the design, for the design as an attempted metaphorical vision is articulated in what it cannot do, in the intensity and scope of its failures. Thomas Sutpen's power is inseparable from his impotence, and it is in understanding this paradox that we may better understand the tension of vitality and deadness in Quentin and all the narrative uncertainties of the "last silence."

Quentin's vision, like Sutpen's, is composed of an intense desire to perceive and the conviction that his perception must fail. His situation is as tortured as Sutpen's because his inheritance is a body of approximations that possess contradictory implications: first, that they are evidence of the progress toward meaning; second, that the very fact that there are only approximations, repeated and sustained, denies the possibility of achieving a meaning.

[6]Our knowledge, from *The Sound and the Fury*, that Quentin commits suicide in the spring of this year is surely relevant here, and would suggest a final relinquishment and "dissolution of the tension."

Absalom, Absalom!

The mode of expression to which Quentin is heir is incredibly powerful; a reader feels that something is always just about to be defined, the heart of the problem revealed. The story which Quentin tells, furthermore, possesses all the more imaginative vitality *because* it is never composed; it is surrounded with countless possible significances; the multiple suggestions by which the story becomes so powerful continue to exist precisely because no single meaning is ever achieved. The vitality of the entire narrative of *Absalom, Absalom!* depends upon the inability to create a single, dominant metaphor; the multiple significances arise out of a permanent stalemate, a failure, a deadness. It is in this way that Thomas Sutpen is most alive because he is dead and that the language of the entire novel is most suggestive of meaning because it constitutes the refutation of a dominant meaning.

As I have attempted to show, it is impossible for Quentin to move beyond a language that is approximate. In his very moments of perception the significances he remarks seem to spring from a denial of meaning and to be given their suggestiveness by the denial, whether it takes the form of the multiple, qualified speculations of all the narrators who have preceded him or that of a hypnotically repeated dialogue that never comes to issue. Quentin's, and a reader's, position regarding the story he tells is always one of uncertainty, where a meaning seems to exist and not to exist. It is ultimately characterized in the relation that Quentin imagines between the men who have come to take Henry Sutpen and Jim Bond, the part Negro idiot who is the last element of the Sutpen story: "They could hear him; he didn't seem to ever get any further away but they couldn't get any nearer and maybe in time they could not even locate the direction any more of the howling" (376). Bond represents the entire story: he is potential meaning, always just out of reach, but asserting in his idiot howling the negation of meaning. The suggestiveness of his presence is denied by the very quality that establishes it, his incomprehensibility. Shreve, with characteristic callousness, reminds Quentin: "...you've got him there still. You still hear him at night sometimes. Don't you?" (378) But a reader is aware that no reminder is necessary, that Bond represents the constant tension that haunts Quentin, the story that must be meaningful and cannot be. For Sutpen, Bond would have been the final symbol of nothingness, the last failure, and he thus embodies the defeat of both narrator and character. He is General Compson's "spirit" crying in the "darkness," and he is a refutation of all that "design," for both Quentin and Sutpen, ever meant.

In my discussions of *Moby-Dick* and "Heart of Darkness," I have frequently remarked Ishmael's and Marlow's reliance upon approximate language of various kinds, from obviously limited special and artificial vocabularies to intensely qualified and just as intensely rendered allusions, reports, and figures. It should be clear now that Quentin Compson, like Marlow, is Ishmael's counterpart in his use of verbal approximations—specifically both in his use of narrative matter taken or inherited from sources outside himself and in his own characteristic imaginative tensions of the artificial and the real, deadness and vitality. It should be clear also that the "last silence" of *Absalom, Absalom!* is equivalent to the "dumb blankness, full of meaning" of *Moby-Dick*. In each case profundity is expressed by the fact that the attempt to achieve profundity must always be qualified, that all the suggestive voices must always be "silent." I have characterized this use of language generally as "simile," in its opposition to the potentially metaphorical visions of Ahab, Kurtz, and Sutpen, and I shall now summarize particularly how the narrative of *Absalom, Absalom!* exhibits its quality as extended simile.

Although the quality of this narrative as simile is most obvious when it is laced with words and phrases like "as though," "perhaps," "I think," and "I would like to believe," and most emphatic when Quentin demonstrates the suggestive failure that all these tags imply, this quality is shown to be a constant property of the entire narrative in that Quentin is the sum of all the narrators and in that the anonymous narrator—in a striking extension of Ishmael's unwillingness to commit himself—refuses to sanction the entire narrative as anything more than hypothesis. The story thus becomes one great "as though" based upon a supposed body of literal details like those of the "Chronology" and "Genealogy" and the attempt to make these details meaningful. All of the narrators attempt to compose these details into a story by which they will become significant both to narrator and listener, and the result is always a suspect relation between literal and metaphorical represented in the approximated story—an extended simile whose assertion of potential meaning insists that such meaning must only be potential. In this way the inability of the imagination to proceed beyond approximation is reflected in both the theme and the method of *Absalom, Absalom!,* and this phenomenon constitutes, I think, the success and the failure of this novel.

In Sutpen's conviction that order lies just beyond his reach and in the constant frustration of his attempts to grasp it, he is himself—like Ahab at the last—a kind of living simile. He represents a distinct kind of language that in his failure is shown to be inadequate. And in his case the simile into which he is transformed is demonstrated to be both the beginning and the end of metaphor, both a step forward to and backward from metaphor. We feel justified in describing him in this way because, as I have suggested previously, both a meaning that he desires and his own sense of its negation are observable in the source and progress of his design. Sutpen's particular negation, furthermore, may be seen to partake of the "darkness" that General Compson holds to be universal and inevitable.

For the narrators of the novel, however, "darkness" is apparent only by reference to the hypothetical story of Sutpen. We are unable, for this reason, to say just why it is that Quentin fails to make the story more than hypothesis. In the case of Sutpen, again, we are presented with a defined and dramatic polarity: "design" and "darkness." His history and his ultimate defeat may be understood in terms of a conflict between these elements. For Quentin there is no such conflict, but only what might be the result of one; the particular vitality-deadness paradox exhibited in his perceptions may well be simply an inherited quality of imagination. Even though his attempt to understand the story is unquestionably genuine, and even though his failure often seems generally persuasive, he may be said to be restricted by his inheritance from previous speakers of both an unresolved story and the conviction that it must remain unresolved. And if we return to these speakers, we find that even here there is no conclusive or even dramatic conflict which decides that the imagination must inevitably fail. The failures of Rosa Coldfield, Quentin's father, and thus of Quentin himself seem at worst a matter of psychology and at best a matter of circumstance, of limitations acting upon them from without and for which they seem not responsible, limitations imposed, of course, by Faulkner. In either case their defeat appears unconvincing as an instance of a defeat to which all men are liable, or as evidence of a "darkness."

The ambiguous problem that the narrators reveal may become generally meaningful, again, in relation to the conflict in Sutpen, but this conflict is not only open to various specific qualifications but also is itself the general product of the narrators' speculations, and we have come full circle. If the inconclusiveness of the narrative is the result of a conflict like the hypothetical struggle of Thomas Sutpen, that conflict does not appear in the narrative except as a creation of and an example of the inconclusiveness itself. The "darkness" itself is only a possibility, and the presentation of imaginative failure as a theme has its ultimate source not in a real tension that is brought to issue in the novel but in the anonymous narrator's declaration that the story may not exist at all. The failure to define a story and to create a metaphor, in other words, seems assumed and lacks force as evidence of the necessity of failure.

For Faulkner, then, the use of extended simile and the defeat it implies becomes the total narrative method: not a dramatized struggle with whatever may lie beyond imagination, and not simply a structural theme that he assumes, but a manner of proceeding that implies that as a theme it is unstable. The fact that the supposed conflict between design and darkness is itself unrealizable may be seen to be an extension of this theme when we consider that Faulkner postulates the failure of *all* metaphor.

This failure was exhibited at the outset in the narratives of Quentin's father and Rosa Coldfield, for the fallibility of both these speakers was expressed in their attempt to transform kinds of disorder, their own inabilities to understand, into metaphor. For Mr. Compson this disorder meant "Fate"; for Rosa it meant Sutpen's "demonhood." In either version the characters of the Sutpen story were shown in futile conflict with something supernatural—in Mr. Compson's case a supernatural force and in Rosa's a supernatural entity. The distinction between these narrators and General Compson, of course, rests in the fact that Quentin's grandfather will postulate only the metaphor of "darkness," but this distinction is not so meaningful as one might suppose, for the "darkness" too suggests the presence of supernatural powers who cannot be defeated. The imaginative failure here thus becomes a metaphor itself, an assertion of the order of the universe, in terms of which Sutpen's defeat is explainable and significant.

This matter may be clarified if we remember that in *Moby-Dick* the ineffable is supposed to have, at least until Ahab finally fails, a metaphorical existence in the white whale and that Melville suggests, in this manner, the reality of a conflict between mind and the ineffable. In "Heart of Darkness," too, we are still dealing—because of Marlow's persistent moral concern—with the "powers of darkness," even though such powers lose significance throughout and the polarity between mind and darkness is, I think, finally destroyed. In both cases the attempts at order are suggested to be meaningful—again, in different degrees —in terms of their conflict with the nature of the universe, with the ineffable.

In *Absalom, Absalom!* the darkness itself—and the metaphorical struggle—is hypothetical. We are thus allowed to question Sutpen's vision of design and nothingness—the vision that causes his failure—and we may even see it as an example of a kind of schizophrenia. In the case of Quentin

Compson, where "darkness" is not even directly suggested, the temptation to use the language of psychopathology is even greater, and we cannot understand why he appears to be the most sympathetically treated narrator. The paradox here is that Quentin seems most psychologically deranged precisely because in terms of the theme of the novel he is most sane: he does not worship the fictions of fate or darkness, but simply, and desperately, confesses that he does not understand. Faulkner suggests in this way that the failure here is just that; it cannot be alleviated or explained by any metaphor, even a metaphor of inevitable failure. In other words, this failure can be displayed conscientiously and realistically only by exhibiting a flat absence of imaginative control and the terrible cost of that absence.

It is for this reason, I think, that Faulkner deliberately places the story beyond his narrators; the essential imaginative problem, he appears to suggest, can be consistently demonstrated only in the failure to create any story at all. No dramatic tensions or conflicts may exist unequivocally in this novel, and we are left with the sheer verbal disorder that reflects the inability to create a fictional world. But the failure to compose a story is the failure to compose a novel, and we have only Faulkner's word that the failure was the unavoidable result of his most conscientious perception, his word for the necessity of defeat.

The last paradox of *Absalom, Absalom!*, then, is the complete interdependence of success with failure in the novel, and this paradox cannot be resolved. That the imagination must fail is not really demonstrated in the novel, and the lack of imaginative control in the novel is, on the one hand, Faulkner's insufficiency. On the other hand, the novel suggests that such a failure could not be demonstrated; it suggests that to resolve the matter by creating a "darkness" is to falsify. This novel is the most thorough-going of those works of fiction that call into question the possibilities of language and meaning; as an immense display of fallen language and as a revelation of the nature of this language, it seems unparalleled. In it Faulkner insists that, as Sutpen's active force and Quentin's imaginative vitality arise from and are exhibited in their failure, the greatest success of language itself is to create a potential of meaning that must remain unrealized, a tension between order and disorder that cannot be resolved but only repeated, and repeated. Language may be defined in this way, however, only because no meaning is ever achieved, because no metaphor is ever constructed.

It is not simply that *Absalom, Absalom!* is possibly one kind of novel or another but that it is possibly no novel at all. Faulkner's insistence that the imagination must fail completely can never be evaluated because it can only remain an insistence. The supposed struggle that it implies could only be revealed metaphorically and thus cannot be revealed—given the insistence—at all. Faulkner's position is superficially equivalent to that of Rosa Coldfield herself, when Rosa questions the metaphors she employs; his assertion that the function of language can only be to create a hypothetical and insoluble potential is *"that true wisdom which can comprehend that there is a might-have-been which is more true than truth"* (143). It may be that Faulkner's inability to dramatize this wisdom, as he suggests, is indicative of a general and inevitable failure of the human mind to order and of his imaginative balance in dealing with this failure; it may be also that, like Rosa, he is not balanced at all, that he is simply unable to allow this wisdom to be tested. There is no way of knowing.

CHAPTER V

Ramifications

AT previous moments in this discussion I have suggested that there is a definite progression to be seen from *Moby-Dick* through "Heart of Darkness" to *Absalom, Absalom!* in terms of each author's concern with the general imaginative difficulty that I have discussed, and I shall now examine this progression in more detail. My purpose is not simply to draw attention to such a development but to show in part how the question of imaginative failure takes form as a problem of method and how the difficulties that it poses have been both emphasized and overcome.

We have seen, first, that the dramatic polarities from which the problem takes its initial expression are continually being broken down, both within a single work and in the three works considered as a hypothetical unit. In *Moby-Dick*, for example, the narrative tension appears to reflect a struggle between language and the ineffable. Ahab's pursuit of something beyond language seems to be sanctioned by Melville to the extent that Ishmael recognizes throughout the book the possibility of a reality beyond the artifices of imagination. Within this recognition, of course, there is a kind of promise that this vague "reality" will be apprehended. The quest for the ineffable is of course perilous, but the expectation of apprehending it often seems real, and it is only at the end of *Moby-Dick* that this expectation is seriously questioned.

It thus appears that the fictional presentation of imaginative failure depends not only upon the sustained recognition and acceptance of language as multiple and complex artifice but also upon a view that is a flat contradiction of this recognition. If the artificiality and multiplicity of imaginative devices are to be evidence of more than simply mortal confusion, if the failure is to be, in fact, a decisive failure, then the expectation of meaning must be strong—so strong as to create the illusion that a failure within language indicates the reality of something beyond language. These expectations, however, contradict the narrator's essential position that such expectations will never be satisfied, that they cannot be satisfied. Melville deals with this paradox by creating a dramatic split down the center of his novel; he insists upon a separation between Ishmael and Ahab. And this separation, in fact, becomes a conflict. *Moby-Dick* does not display a struggle between Ahab and the white whale or between man and "Truth" so much as a conflict between two kinds of consciousness and two sorts of language—Ishmael's suggestive and ultimately centerless multiplicity against Ahab's rigid and intense expectation of the one revelation.

The ambivalence of Melville's attitude toward Ahab may now be understood. If Ishmael's willingness to admit countless possibilities is to be meaningful as a failure of imagination in conflict with the inexpressible, and not simply as confusion, then Ahab's position must be both significant and nonsensical; Melville must both accept and reject him. Without Ahab as potential seer the unstructured artifice of the narrative would be indicative only of aimless complexity; without Ahab as monomaniac the complexity would be destroyed by a simplifying moment of vision.

My conclusions that Ahab's death is not tragic, that he cannot be accepted on his own terms, and that he seems a ritual sacrifice to Melville's convictions may also be extended. Ahab is an implement to Melville's purpose; he is the incarnation of the uncertain promise of fulfillment, of meaningful resolution, that Ishmael's narrative technique both implies and denies. The denial, at the last, is definite; Ahab dies in conflict with what might simply be a whale, and he might not, therefore, be representative of a metaphorical attempt to attain the meaning within—he might not be significant at all.

And yet the sustaining of the possibility of the metaphorical vision up to Ahab's death allows Melville to employ apparently all the languages at his command and contend that what he has in mind is still uncommunicated, that it is, indeed, inexpressible. It is the tension that Ahab represents that renders Ishmael's rhetoric so powerful, this tension that convinces a reader that a genuine attempt to express something beyond words is being made. The vitality of Ahab lends an intensity to Ishmael's language that it otherwise would not have, and certainly one of the effects of Ahab's ultimate failure—although, as I have said, this failure is totally ambiguous—is dramatically to emphasize this intensity. For Ahab has served his purpose. The attempt to know, we feel, has been made. The complicated artifice of Ishmael's rhetoric is the indication of something beyond rhetoric, and Ahab's failure—the final impossibility of knowing—is Melville's success.

In this way what I have called the "dramatic polarities"

of the problem of imaginative failure, the presentation of a conflict between mind and some inexpressible reality, depend upon a paradoxically divided attitude toward the capacities of language, upon the continued expectation that meaning will and must be achieved in spite of the continued suggestion that it cannot be. Such ambivalence is not, of course, durable; the conclusion of *Moby-Dick* serves to deny completely the possibility of metaphorical perception, and—although it is most suggestive in terms of the expectations that have preceded it—in itself this denial not only reasserts the inadequacy of language but also refutes the idea that such inadequacy may become suggestive of anything beyond language and thus of meaningful failure itself. The nature of the paradox, in other words, is defined at the end of *Moby-Dick;* it is there that the crucial question regarding imaginative failure is raised, and the idea of something ineffable about human experience that justifies imaginative failure seems to depend upon the fact that this question does occur at the conclusion, that it is not pursued.

If we turn to "Heart of Darkness," however, we discover that the ambivalent vision upon which the idea of the ineffable rests is apparent throughout the story in Marlow's own divided imagination. The desperation of Marlow's attempts to achieve a meaning arises from his inability to tolerate the sort of arbitrariness that Ishmael represents. For Marlow, Kurtz's voice is a crucial example of the hollow multiplicity of human disciplines, and Kurtz's fall is the inevitable consequence of the disparity between this multiplicity and a supposed reality.

Because the superficiality of Kurtz's and his own "reality" threatens him with moral collapse, Marlow must adopt, rather than simply entertain, a self-contradictory attitude analogous to Ahab's; he must feel that the fictional quality of the kinds of order upon which he has relied indicates the existence of something beyond this order—a darkness. But, unlike *Moby-Dick,* "Heart of Darkness" does not end here. Marlow's moral being depends upon apprehending the ineffable, upon illuminating the darkness, and, unlike Ahab, he is able to pursue the matter and survive.

It may be added, too, that Marlow's moral concerns— his desperate search for solidity of some sort—are, like the figure of Ahab, the means by which the confusions of his own rhetoric become so suggestive; a reader feels that the darkness exists and that it will finally be illuminated precisely because Marlow seems so dependent upon it. The difficulty of achieving a meaning seems evidence only of the dimensions of this meaning. But the cost of such suggestiveness, of pursuing the darkness with such persistence, is great, and it is great just because the pursuit of the ineffable can only emphasize the tenuousness of its foundations. On the one hand, Marlow asserts that the artificiality of his "realities" indicates the existence of a "darkness"; on the other hand, his attempt to pursue the darkness is completely unsatisfied, and he discovers not a darkness but simply nothing at all. The result is his despair, and this despair is significant in its striking contrast to the dominant tone of *Moby-Dick.*

Whereas Melville's "whiteness"—the multiple and qualified implications of Ishmael's narrative, the artificial complexity of language itself—seems for the most part indicative of some inexpressible order that gives imaginative failure significance, Conrad's "darkness" is most often the obvious expression of Marlow's confusion: it is a moral euphemism for the vacancy of Marlow's experience, for his inability to discover anything at the supposed center of things. The idea that the only possible "order" depends upon the inadequacy of order is to Marlow intolerable. He cannot endure the kind of ambiguity that became apparent at the end of *Moby-Dick*. His attempts to resolve the matter, however, serve to destroy the conception of even an ineffable reality, for he discovers only emptiness. The "darkness" dissolves. Marlow must be tenacious, and the slightest imaginative tenacity is completely destructive.

Marlow's attempt to apprehend the darkness, in this way, serves essentially to emphasize the paradox upon which the idea of an "ineffable" depends: that the inconclusiveness of one's discoveries and the denial of one's expectations is itself a meaningful discovery. It becomes clear in "Heart of Darkness" that the idea of an ineffable reality like Marlow's "darkness" can exist only if one does not make an unequivocal attempt to establish it, only if one is not forced by his own demands to observe that its existence depends wholly upon a failure—a failure to create a "reality" within language. If one is not content to accept the unreality of his imaginative pursuits as such —and Marlow cannot be—then he must attempt to move beyond language by means of the inadequacies of language. Such a movement can be suggested, but it depends, in fact, upon remaining only a suggestive manner of speaking. The idea of the significance of the inexpressible can survive only so long as one does not commit himself to it. The penalty for such a commitment is not death, as in *Moby-Dick,* but total imaginative confusion.

The ambivalence of Marlow's vision—his assertion of the existence of a darkness despite his awareness that it is founded only upon the emptiness of his "realities"— becomes most apparent because of his demands for moral certainty, and this ambivalence demonstrates also the thoroughness of Conrad's preoccupation with the problem of imaginative failure. The conflict between imagination and the ineffable has been shown itself to be unreal, to be dependent upon a paradox that is insupportable. A pursuit that begins with a dissatisfaction with the powers of language turns upon itself, and the possibility of a meaning beyond linguistic inadequacy can only be defined in terms of the inadequacy with which one began. The effect of this, of course, is to undercut the significance of the problem, since the pursuit of the inexpressible only emphasizes the expressed confusions of its sources. In "Heart of Darkness," in other words, the failure of language is most emphatically a failure; its issue is not the "ineffable," but the confusion in which it originates.

It may be helpful to put this another way: the tensions of the works of fiction that I have considered become increasingly the tensions of language. In *Moby-Dick* a reader's attention is drawn to the multiplicity, the arbitrariness, and the artificiality of language. The sort of expectations exhibited in the figure of Ahab, however, create the illusion of an actual conflict between language and some ineffable reality, which could be called "life" or "truth."

Melville's ability to pose the question in these terms depends upon the fact that Ahab dies at the end of his narrative, that our expectations of meaning are established in the narrative and only questioned seriously at the last. In "Heart of Darkness," Marlow's—and a reader's—expectations are questioned much sooner and with much more intensity. The narrator's moral concerns and his scrutiny of the sort of "reality" that he can command have the consequence—largely because of their persistence—of calling into question even the inexpressible synthesis that "darkness" implies. Language, in other words, is seen in conflict with an emptiness: the realities of the ordering imagination are not simply unreal; they are hollow. We discover that the idea of a darkness does nothing but describe our reaction to the vacancy at the center of things. And without the benefit of an illusory conflict between language and some ineffable reality, the matter becomes a question of the imagination in conflict with itself. Marlow's inability to illuminate the meaning at the center of things serves as a vaguely allegorical demonstration of the inability to create a certain kind of metaphor—a metaphor that implies the greatest imaginative activity or movement; "meaning at the center" loses its suggestive power, and the dramatic conflict between language and something else, again, dissolves.

The problem of imagination now becomes a problem of using language in certain ways—a matter within an individual imaginative consciousness—so as to control the artificiality and arbitrariness that the slightest inquisitiveness reveals. It is significant that whereas in *Moby-Dick* and "Heart of Darkness" the narrative structure is that of the search or hunt, in *Absalom, Absalom!* the "story" is just an account of various ways of talking. The search is a search for a kind of language by means of language. For the central character and the narrators of *Absalom, Absalom!*, the problem becomes that of reducing a complexity of public significances to a controlled structure of certain and personal order; Sutpen, for example, attempts to make a world of significances a part of himself, to make its relation to himself unquestionable by composing it in a rigorous and unequivocal manner.

That Sutpen, in making this attempt, is attempting to create metaphor itself becomes clear when we consider the characteristic gestures of his struggle. These are presented as comprising a total act of assimilation and reduction; Sutpen must accumulate as many possessions as he can while constantly making sure that these possessions are significant in only one way, that they are part of a consistent whole. The "possessions" of the narrators of *Absalom, Absalom!*, to pursue the analogy, are simply various kinds of language. These narrators must attempt to subsume various and contradictory vocabularies or systems of implications into a single, consistent language that—because it is unified and unambiguous—will become a metaphor for the meaning of their own experience and perhaps for all experience. Their failure—like Sutpen's failure to control the ambiguities of his acquisitions—is expressed as the failure to establish final connections between disparate kinds of language, connections that would serve as at least a beginning in the process of reducing the artificial multiplicity of language to a single and therefore significant language, to a code that will be relevant to all human experience.

In the works that I have considered to this point we may note the continual struggle to establish connections among disparate languages, and the central characters and narrators of these works continually suggest the possibility of moving from the language of the "exterior" to that of the "interior." They suggest that these languages are fundamentally different, but they are sure that some connection may be made. It is occasionally suggested in "Heart of Darkness," for example—as it is in the idea that Ahab's language in *Moby-Dick* is "untraditional"—that there is a language of the center, or of the depths or the heights, and that through intense imaginative efforts, the language or reality of "surfaces" will become this language of the "heart," a language that will express reality or life or truth, or at least will demonstrate a more intimate connection between some reality and the human mind and thus alleviate the complex artificiality with which Marlow begins. The dissolution of the supposed conflict between mind and the ineffable, of course, is also the dissolution of the possibility of this mysterious "other" vocabulary. And in the emphasis that the central figures place upon "surfaces" or seemingly irrelevant details, it is perhaps apparent that such a distinct and ultimate language never existed at all, even as a possibility. Ahab's attempt to achieve meaning, for example, is by means of the apparent refutations of meaning: by a certain kind of concentration upon appearances he will transform them into a reality. When we arrive at Sutpen's treatment of a similar matter, furthermore, and consider that he attempts to transform the social structure by means of that structure, we may understand that his attempt is representative of the general struggle to move beyond language by means of language, both to accumulate languages and to reduce them and thereby to control the meaning of experience unequivocally.

This inability to connect one sort of language with another may not, then, be defined simply as an inability to move from simpler vocabularies to more abstract and supposedly more "meaningful" ways of talking—vocabularies, for example, of morality or God or love. The failure is a failure to establish unequivocally the connection between any two vocabularies as a beginning in the process of constructing the "one language," whose consistency and universality will indicate its quality as a dominant or potentially dominant metaphorical order.

The idea of reducing and controlling the multiplicity of language is simply another way of expressing the process of creating metaphor, and the failure to establish connections between various kinds of language is the failure to render experience meaningful by means of metaphor. The result of this failure, as we have seen, takes the form of an insistence upon the value of the simile and the conviction that only the simile can be sustained. The simile, of course, is fundamentally associated with the attempt to establish relations between disparate vocabularies, with the object of creating a single language that will be generally meaningful. The approximations of the simile, in terms of our expectations, should result in a reduction of the disparate elements of a comparison to a metaphorical consistency. The fact that approximation and disparity are merely sustained and never resolved in a writer such as Faulkner indicates not only that such consistency cannot be realized but also, by virtue of the insistence upon the simile, that the expectation of it is always unjustifiable. And, again, with the dissolution of this expectation, the illusion of a disparity between language and something beyond language dwindles to a problem contained within language; the only significant disparity is expressed in the separateness of the multiple implications of words and vocabularies themselves. The idea of an nonverbal reality has disappeared, and the creation of a composed verbal reality has become impossible. The sustaining of the simile is significant as an insistence upon linguistic disorder, and it is this disorder—which can imply neither success nor failure—that comes to be representative of an imaginative difficulty that was formerly a matter of a dramatic conflict between distinct polarities.

The nature of the inexpressible as something to be skirted around or directly assailed is shown to be only another artifice of imagination, and the implication is that the most realistic expression of the problem is to admit one's confusion, to confess the inability to construct any sort of consistent and unified order that will not reveal its nature as exclusive artifice. With the collapse of the expectations of ultimate significance appears the collapse of the conception of a reality beyond language that renders the inadequacy of language meaningful, but the convictions that language is artificial and, furthermore, that language as a whole contains systems of implications that are so many and so discrete as to refute even the possibility of synthesis or unification—these convictions persist. As a consequence, the attempt to achieve order results not in a mystery, but in a muddle. The stature of imagination is questioned.

In the preceding section I have remarked the dissolution of the ability to present the problem as a significant conflict. I have occasionally used the word "dramatic" to describe this conflict, and I have done so deliberately, for the collapse of the structural polarities by which the imaginative difficulty may be meaningfully depicted transforms the problem into that of using language in a certain way and thus into a narrative, rather than a dramatic, problem. The essential result of this collapse, in other words, takes the form of an insistence upon the reality and immediacy of the narrator himself, upon the problematic quality of the artistic structure or structurer, and it is just this sort of insistence that is the most pervasive and consistent preoccupation of most of the late nineteenth and twentieth century novelists now generally assumed to be important.

This is not simply a matter, again, of the phenomenon that the most important characters in the particular works I have considered are the narrators of those works, although this is certainly true. It is a matter of the reader's attention being drawn, in much modern fiction, to narrative method by means of narrative disorder, whether this disorder be, for example, temporal or psychological. Literary criticism has not failed to recognize this preoccupation with narrative difficulties, but it has too frequently assumed, for instance, that the confused narrative—of which the "stream of consciousness" technique is a primary example—is presented as the best possible means of either defining the tempo and complexity of "modern experience" or displaying the wonderful activity of the mind itself. I do not wish to construct a neat generalization here, but I would suggest that narrative disorder may often imply, quite simply, the unintelligibility of it all and that the confused narrative is often indicative not of a writer's conviction of success but of his preoccupation with imaginative failure.

It should be unnecessary to add here that of course the concentration in fiction upon the failures and successes of a narrator does not exhaust the possible expressions of the sort of imaginative disintegration that I am describing. Although I have not pursued this matter with any thoroughness beyond Melville, Conrad, and Faulkner, even a cursory consideration of other writers may reveal the differing ramifications that a dissatisfaction with the possibilities of imaginative creation may have.[1] If we return for a moment to *Moby-Dick*, we may remember that there the

[1]The likeliest possibilities for pursuit here would seem to be—of the better known novelists—Ford Madox Ford, Virginia Woolf, E. M. Forster, D. H. Lawrence, and James Joyce. I do not mean to suggest that the idea of imaginative failure is necessarily as significant, as central, or as defined in these writers as it is in Melville, Conrad, and Faulkner, but only that it is usually involved in a fundamental way.

burden of incoherency rests in Ishmael's narrative consciousness and that Ahab functions as the possibility of rendering the narrative finally coherent—a possibility that is shown, of course, to be unreal. In general, the presentation of the problem requires such a disparity between coherency and incoherency, but the location of the elements of this disparity may vary. That is to say that it does not really matter whether a general narrative structurelessness is superimposed upon characters and segments of "experience" that are supposedly ultimately consistent and unified or whether an apparently potential narrative order is played off against characters and experiences whose ambiguities continually seem to refute it.

In theoretical expression, this distinction may well seem tenuous, but it becomes more comprehensible if we consider *Moby-Dick* or *Absalom, Absalom!,* in which the narrative structure itself implies unintelligibility, as opposed to *Ulysses,* in which the main structural principle seems perfectly coherent in itself, but also—in relation to the imagined experience the novel contains—perfectly arbitrary. The "order" that results is for the most part one of irony and not, I think, the sort of irony that leads us to some unified view of human experience. The superimposing of the experience of the myth upon the experience of modern Dublin has the basic effect of emphasizing the disorder of modern experience—not simply the antiheroicalness of it, but the meaninglessness of it—and the arbitrariness of the myth in relation to it. The narratives within the mythical structure, furthermore, the various formalized linguistic techniques of the individual episodes, may be seen as a great display of the centerlessness and multiplicity of the possible linguistic perspectives at one's command. In this way Joyce's episodes are exactly parallel to the chapters of *Moby-Dick;* they serve primarily to exhibit the richness and also the arbitrariness and discreteness of the particular vocabularies that are open to the supposed structurer or structure.[2]

Another example of this method—of the use of an insistent "structure" that, in conjunction with the complexities of the imagined world to which it is applied, serves mainly to emphasize its limitations—may be found in the works of D. H. Lawrence, although Lawrence accomplishes this sort of unintelligibility, as I see it, in a much less deliberate and self-conscious manner than either Joyce or the novelists that I have considered at length. The details of Lawrence's general practice are summed up nicely by Robert M. Adams:

...the structure of his [Lawrence's] novels is not, ordinarily, open to any notable degree. The narrative may be, and usually is, fairly primitive; but it achieves the modicum of resolution normal in the modern novel. Its episodes may be loosely joined or altogether unconnected on the level of mechanical causation but are usually broadly linked in terms of someone's psychological development. And in fact it is in their concept of character that Lawrence's novels are most interestingly open. Fluid, violent, demanding, inconsistent, and direct, the characters of Lawrence have a vitality which refuses to be fixed; their sense

[2]In his account of the manner in which Joyce manipulated the raw materials of *Ulysses,* Robert M. Adams demonstrates that the focus upon meaninglessness in that novel is not, as I have suggested, simply a matter of the disparity between mythical parallels and the narrative, but a matter of a disparity between a great many of the narrative details and any sort of symbolic intention or pattern. Adams remarks at one point, for example, that "many of the changes that Joyce imposed upon the raw materials of his book and some of the selections that he made among them are designed to confuse or blur, rather than to create or emphasize patterns." *Surface and Symbol* (New York: Oxford University Press, 1962), p. 244.

of life as pattern is weak, their sense of impulse and need very strong. In the rituals of private religion they achieve various provisional and temporary fulfillments; but beyond and beneath all forms their allegiance is to something fluid and impermanent, so that, unless they are mere allegorical abstractions, one never feels them capable of, or interested in, any sort of settlement with life. There is a level of existence beneath ideas and institutions, beyond thought and speech and literature itself, after which they are always groping. They proclaim an inward grace of which no adequate outer sign really exists and which Lawrence can suggest only by their flaring, nervous, irritable speech. The chief quality of his characters is their sensitivity or lack of sensitivity to a set of mysterious interior variables; the chief quality which the novels themselves cultivate is sensitivity and intensity of response.[3]

I have little to add to this account save a brief attempt to relate Lawrence to the critical terminology that I have developed. Occasionally Lawrence may be seen to rely heavily upon a perfectly coherent set of psychological metaphors—metaphors so coherent, in fact, that they sometimes threaten to destroy the complexity of a given narrative world. I have in mind here the nearly formulaic Oedipal implications—in *Sons and Lovers*—of Paul's fluctuation between his mother and Miriam and of the sort of solution to the problem that Clara Dawes represents, a solution that becomes unnecessary when his mother dies. The emphatic neatness of such a reading, itself, would render it suspect, even if the characters themselves—in the incredible intensity and perhaps the formlessness of their actions and reactions—did not often seem to overthrow completely the

[3]*Strains of Discord: Studies in Literary Openness* (Ithaca: Cornell University Press, 1958), p. 189.

pat psychological scheme in which they appear to be placed.

More characteristic of Lawrence, however, is the sort of mythical and metaphorical "system" that is only half-expressed, the "system" that depends upon ultimately opaque central metaphors like the ideas of the blood and the visceralness of life or upon extended descriptions of what are presumably human beings in electrical or neurological or, more generally, primarily inorganic terms. Sets of metaphors like these, I think, do not appear pursuable to a reader, especially when one considers the nervous frequency with which they replace one another and the often arbitrary manner in which Lawrence may present them. But Lawrence himself seems to know what he means; in fact, he insists that he does: he insists that there is a real language toward which his not quite coherent or stable figures are working. But this insistence may be all there is. Lawrence might even be said in this connection to substitute changing rhythmical intensities for verbal patterns. The "order" of a novel like *Women in Love* may be only his passionate and incantatory certainty that order is there behind or within the discrete, erratic, and brittle impulses of his confident and essentially confusing metaphorical "patterns."

The parallel in American literature to the use of mythical patterns and pseudopatterns in Joyce and Lawrence is, of course, the technique of William Faulkner, but this parallel should remind us mainly of differences. For it is in Faulkner, as in Conrad, Virginia Woolf, and Ford, that we frequently find an intense focus upon the individual consciousness struggling to create order—as opposed to the remote juxtaposition of available structures or to the violent assertion of a certain but incoherent and possibly private "order"—and it is here that the idea of imaginative failure becomes most complex and its consequences most meaningful and most severe.[4]

Faulkner's attempt to create a mythology, again, provides an excellent example. The complexities of specific and confused stories in Faulkner may often be referred to a vague historical mythology of Yoknapatawpha County or of the entire South. The illusion of meaning arises from the vague notions that the place of an action or a speech is the same as that of many other perhaps equally discrete and confused actions or speeches. By this means, specific confusions are suggested to be part of a larger fabric that seems meaningful.[5] I have suggested in my treatment of *Absalom, Absalom!*, however, that Faulkner's myth is never really established except in such a way as to emphasize its quality as artifice and arbitrary artifice at that: the myth is unstable.

If a writer does not employ the defined and finally remote sort of structure that we may observe in *Ulysses* or even in the ambiguous presentation of Ahab in *Moby-Dick*, if—like Faulkner—he attempts to create his own formal or metaphorical frame or to demonstrate the failure of order by exhibiting the struggle for it in an individual consciousness, then the presentation of imaginative failure becomes

[4]Regarding Ford, I am thinking of *The Good Soldier; Parade's End*, for example, is a more complicated matter, although it nonetheless bears relation to the problem as I see it.

[5]Faulkner often attempts to achieve this kind of unity in single narratives by attempting to destroy the temporal or grammatical order of a story with rhetorical confusion. He may suggest, for example, that all action is part of a single great action which, because it is *one*, is meaningful. The best example of this is a characteristic Faulknerian rhetorical gesture: A did Z as B was to do Y when C did X, not knowing even then that D had done W though E, and so on.

largely inseparable from the presentation of sheer linguistic disorder. The most conscientious recognition of the possible failure of imagination necessitates narrative techniques that are antithetical not only to the traditional means and ends of the novel but also to any sort of intelligibility or coherency. When linguistic confusion becomes the most realistic expression of the conditions of language and experience, then the foundations of the novel begin to crumble.

One obvious reason for this collapse is that a narrative constructed upon the principle of utter disorder may be just unreadable, a progression of unrealized tensions, imperfect images, and faulty metaphors. Even if we could understand the function of such imperfections, the experience of reading might involve simply the continual recognition of variously and carefully constructed flaws. Their insistent centerlessness might destroy, perhaps, what Conrad calls one's "belief in mankind"; it would certainly destroy one's faith in art.

But there is a less fastidious objection to pursuing the possibilities of imaginative failure. The appreciation of the novel of failure as such depends upon reading it within a meaningful frame, within a tradition; it depends, in short, upon assuming at the outset that the confusion of the narrative has a certain meaning, and this assumption, as I see it, can never be justified.

The crux of this matter lies in the ambiguity of a novelist such as Faulkner—the fundamental ambiguity between a supposedly self-conscious presentation of the essential imaginative difficulty and the particular and unself-conscious confusions of the novelist himself. I have remarked previously that we are often tempted to use the language of psychopathology about Faulkner's characters, but then

—because these characters seem to be representative of the entire world of a given novel—we transfer these psychological labels to all the characters, to the narrator or narrators, or to the author himself.

Sutpen's "schizophrenia," for example, the split between his fanatical assertion of his identity and his conviction that he has and can have no identity, is also the dominant quality of the narrators of the novel, whose metaphorical visions are always accompanied by their implicit contradictions. The supposed psychoses of both character and narrators are expressed in this way. They are expressed in an attempt to achieve a metaphorical vision of the world—and again I would emphasize that the nature of this vision as aberration is defined not in its particular details but in the insistence that it is unambiguous, in its metaphorical intensity—and in the recognition of the futility of this attempt, a futility that results from the recognition of disorder as somehow permanent.

It is just this kind of split vision, moreover, that is necessary to the meaningful presentation of the imaginative problem. If the failure is to be significant, to appear as anything more than sustained confusion, then the expectations of order must be real—paradoxically real in view of the necessary recognition of disorder. Melville, as we have seen, solves this problem by transforming this imaginative split into an artistic dichotomy—Ishmael and Ahab —that is seen to be completely artificial only at the last. Joyce may be said to solve the problem by creating a similarly artistic and artificial division—although the expectations created by such a flat division are not strong—the division between the myth and the fictional life. In these terms the insistence upon failure in "Heart of Darkness" and the sustained complexity of *Absalom, Absalom!* are the result of an artificial, technical split becoming personal; the assertion of order and the recognition of disorder become paradoxically contained in the single consciousness of Marlow or of Quentin Compson.

If this is a failure of technique, however, it has its justification. *Moby-Dick* has demonstrated with great intensity the dissolution of order and the tenuous artificiality of expectations of order; it may well be that these expectations no longer exist, for Conrad or Faulkner, as real possibilities and that therefore they can only be expressed as the paradoxical bent of some individual consciousness; as such, again, they may appear a kind of insanity.

The insanity of Ahab or Sutpen, of course, is clearly of greater dimensions than that of Ishmael or Quentin. It may be defined as the assertion of order in the face of disorder, in which the intensity of the assertion is directly proportional, it appears, to the pervasiveness of the confusion. Sanity, on the other hand, becomes either the flat and despairing recognition of disorder or—and this is more likely—a recognition that the imagination must always deal with its ambiguities in a qualified manner. This latter position, of which Marlow is often an example, involves the recognition of ultimate defeat but also a dogged persistence and attempt to "make do." It involves, also, a kind of "as if" thinking, whereby one continually attempts to order experience with the sense that no final commitment to any such attempt is possible, with the awareness that imaginative structure is "necessary fiction." This is the sort of attitude that we encounter, for example, in much twentieth century poetry, and though it is unquestionably "sane," it often suggests a lack of vitality, a hollow sort of intellectualizing. The expectation of order, although possibly insane, is necessary if the problems of imagination are to seem important.[6]

Because such "insanity" may seem to become the rule of a fictional world, a reader may hesitate to see this world as relevant to the world at large. And if the author appears to demand such relevance—as he usually does in the act of writing and presenting the novel—then he too becomes suspect. Faulkner's presentation of imaginative failure, in these terms, may seem the product of his own psychological difficulties.

It is natural for us to demand order and significance of the novel, not simply because it is traditional to do so but because of our ever-present appetite for significance of any sort. The denial of this appetite may be unacceptable; we may tend to isolate a novelist's insistence upon defeat from the world at large by using the most efficient means at our command for accomplishing such isolation—psychopathological language. Each novel that Faulkner writes does not assume the relevance that novels usually are held to possess but becomes another chapter in his case history.

The inescapable and destructive paradox here is that by viewing a novelist's assertion of the need for order and his postulation of the permanence of disorder as psychologically suspect, we ignore the problem that he *may* be exhibiting just because we share his supposed psychological problem. If we insist that sustained disorder is unreason-

[6]It is worth noting here that at the end of Chapter II I suggested that the distinctions between Ishmael and Ahab may be observed, because of the disappearance of the ineffable, to become blurred. Here I would like to invert the proposition, for this is a case of reciprocal causes rather than cause and effect. As I shall show later, the merging of these characters may itself be seen as the cause of the disappearance of the ineffable and the emphasis upon nothingness.

able or unreal, then we do not see that in doing so we are ourselves examples of the "insanity" that he may be dramatizing, the insanity that is the fundamental quality of imagination: the insistence upon significances, the assumption of unambiguous meaning in experience that—as the novelist suggests—is inseparable from the confrontation of the confusion of experience. I hasten to add that such a novelist may not be significant in these terms, and, furthermore, that we may have no way whatsoever, in a single novel, of knowing whether the confusion that he presents is representative confusion or simply confusion, no way of knowing—in the most thorough and realistic presentation of imaginative failure that we encounter in Faulkner—whether the novelist is making any assertion at all.[7]

The problem possesses more complexities, certainly, than these, but one general conclusion—considering the example of William Faulkner—seems unavoidable: to pursue the matter of imaginative failure, to demonstrate that the greatest imaginative control is to admit a total lack of control, is at worst to stop writing novels and at best to insist that novels cannot be written. For the single possible justification for the conviction that the imagination must fail to structure its perceptions—if the problem is taken to its extreme—must rest upon hypothetical patterns that are never resolved, upon dramatic conflicts that can never take place, and, above all, upon the persistent unreality of the expectation that could make the confusion meaningful, the expectation of a possible order.

[7]Wayne Booth sketches the possibility of such problems. *The Rhetoric of Fiction* (Chicago, 1961), pp. 297–98.

CHAPTER VI

The Range of the Problem

IN the following pages I shall discuss other works by Melville, Conrad, and Faulkner that appear to be immediately relevant to the imaginative problem I have described. I present short accounts of these works not primarily as evidence of each author's concern with the problem—for the preceding chapters are the best evidence for that which I can give—but as examples of the various forms that such a preoccupation may take. I shall confine myself to exhibiting in brief the general structure and central patterns of images of these works, and it may be that my treatment of them, in terms of the preceding discussions, will seem overly simple. It is possible, also, that more extended treatments of these works would not reach identical conclusions with or even take the same form as my discussions of *Moby-Dick,* "Heart of Darkness," and *Absalom, Absalom!* But at the same time it would be tiresome and unnecessary, both for a reader and myself, to pursue these works as far as I have my main examples. It is my intention to show only that, in relation to the complex of attitudes I have called the "failure of imagination," the texture of these other works is familiar, that the possibility of pursuit is there.

The conclusion that Melville's *Pierre* fails as a novel seems unavoidable, but the manner of its failure is important. Melville is intent upon rendering Pierre's decline and fall as evidence of the possibility of all human collapse given the presence in life of insoluble "ambiguities," but it is difficult for a reader, despite Melville's insistence, to view Pierre in this light. The hero's naïve impulsiveness in responding to the supposed fact that Isabel is his illegitimate half-sister, his certainty that she presents a mystery that is unknowable, and his general inability to deal with the supposed problem that she represents do not seem the results of the inevitable nature of things. And along with the responsibility for failure that we may assign to Pierre —his particular folly—we may postulate as reasons for his fall the suggested enticements and horrors of incest, and while it is remarkable in a novel that appeared in 1852, this psychological question tends to define the failure even more emphatically as particular and individual: if not a matter of folly, it may be a matter of sickness.

By far the most important qualification of the relevance of Pierre's failure, however, is the pervasive malignity that opposes him in the world of the novel, for it seems that this world is not ambiguous at all, but simply evil. The story is reminiscent of the work of Thomas Hardy, for Melville appears just as relentless as Hardy can be in his insistence that his central character must fail, that it is a fatal universe, and that only the most horrible end is possible.

But although Pierre's progress toward destruction is not satisfactorily rendered in terms of the "ambiguities," Melville is nonetheless certain that insolubility is the dominant fact of human experience. The narrator's remarks are always most valuable as articulations of the problem that was so suggestively presented in *Moby-Dick:*

But the vague revelation was now in him, that the visible world, some of which before had seemed but too common and prosaic to him; and but too intelligible; he now vaguely felt, that all the world, and every misconceivedly common and prosaic thing in it, was steeped a million fathoms in a mysteriousness wholly hopeless of solution. (150)

Like all youths, Pierre had conned his novel-lessons; had read more novels than most persons of his years; but their false, inverted attempts at systematizing eternally unsystemizable elements; their audacious, intermeddling impotency, in trying to unravel...the more thin than gossamer threads which make up the complex web of life....He saw that human life doth truly come from that, which all men are agreed to call by the name of *God;* and that it partakes of the unravelable inscrutableness of God. (165–166)

In those Hyperborean regions, to which enthusiastic Truth, and Earnestness, and Independence, will invariably lead a mind fitted by nature for profound and fearless thought, all objects are seen in a dubious, uncertain, and refracting light. Viewed through that rarefied atmosphere the most immemorially admitted maxims of men begin to slide and fluctuate, and finally become wholly inverted....(194)[1]

In all these passages the elusiveness of "truth" is emphasized; a man's struggles after such truth inevitably reveals only Ishmael-like uncertainty and results in an admonition characteristic of Ishmael: "...it is not for man to follow the trail of truth too far" (194). And whereas in *Moby-Dick* the reality of such truth is completely questioned only at the last, in *Pierre* the matter is taken farther; although

[1]Herman Melville, *Pierre or, The Ambiguities,* ed. Henry A. Murray (New York: Hendricks House, 1949).

The Range of the Problem

Pierre could not be seen as an Ahab, Melville demands that his experience should be defined similarly:

...because Pierre began to see through the first superficiality of the world, he fondly weens he has come to the unlayered substance. But, far as any geologist has yet gone down into the world, it is found to consist of nothing but surface stratified on surface. To its axis, the world being nothing but superinduced superficies. By vast pains we mine into the pyramid; by horrible gropings we come to the central room; with joy we espy the sarcophagus; but we lift the lad—and no body is there!—appallingly vacant as vast is the soul of man. (335)[2]

In this passage Melville characterizes the matter of the "surface" and the "reality" in a way that may be seen to anticipate the particular hollowness of Kurtz and the general absence of all meaning dramatized in "Heart of Darkness," as well as the suggestive struggle within and for nothingness to be found in *Absalom, Absalom!* We may note that the possibility of some inexpressible reality that

[2]Compare Melville's statement of the problem to Kenneth Burke's. In speaking of Robert Penn Warren's *Night Rider*, Burke remarks: "First, it seems to me an unusually beautiful novel written in what I would call the 'to the end of the line' mode. At one point, for instance, the process of maturing is metaphorically described as the peeling away of the successive layers of an onion, which would perfectly suggest such development by introversion, by inturning towards a nonexistent core, as I would consider typical of the 'to the end of the line' kind of plot." A few pages later he refers suggestively to *Moby-Dick* in the same terms: "We should also note a 'serial' quality in the 'to the end of the line' mode—a kind of 'withinness of withinness,'...And in *Moby-Dick* there is an especially efficient passage of this sort, prophetically announcing the quality of Ishmael's voyage: after walking through 'blocks of blackness,' he enters a door where he stumbles over an ash box; going on, he finds that he is in a Negro church, and 'the preacher's text was about the blackness of darkness.'" *The Philosophy of Literary Form* (New York: Random House, Inc., 1957), pp. 71, 74.

was so striking in *Moby-Dick* is here conspicuously absent. The reward of a supposedly penetrating vision of the world and of a descent into the self is simply nothingness. It seems likely, moreover, that *Pierre* lacks force as a novel precisely because Melville was attempting to present something that could not be presented, that his awareness of "ambiguities" could not be dramatized because he was convinced of their ultimate lack of significance—convinced of the vacancy upon which they seem to rest.

In *Pierre,* to put this another way, the expectation of an ultimate vision is totally unreal; the failure of the protagonist is even more ritualistically sacrificial than that of Ahab, and as a failure it is much less suggestive. There is no struggle for the discovery of some ineffable reality; Pierre himself becomes simply an example for Melville's implacable assertion of the impossibility of any sort of imaginative success. The result is both a confusion without complexity and an insistent "fatality" of the sort we have come to associate with Jason Compson III.

The Confidence-Man is a better book, or perhaps its faults are more palatable. It begins with a dramatic polarity: the "lamb-like" man, a deaf-mute dressed in "cream-colors," boards the Mississippi steam ship "Fidele" and displays upon a slate various exhortations to "charity," whereupon a barber hangs out a sign in the shape of an opened razor which proclaims "No Trust." The remainder of the narrative serves, rather than to resolve this polarity one way or the other, to reassert continually the tension between trust and distrust.

The problem of this novel will seem familiar to readers of *Moby-Dick;* it is that of penetrating the multiple appearances of the natural and supernatural in human life to some sort of meaningful assertion about life, to a reality.

These appearances are the various identities of what is apparently—and incredibly—a single character, the confidence man, and they are always subject to at least two possible interpretations: the confidence man is a fraud and, perhaps—given his fantastic mutability—a devil who preys upon those he can deceive, or he is a kind of Christ figure who succors man by instilling in him the healing virtues of hope and confidence. Both the supernatural aspect of the confidence man and the crucial intensity of focus upon the matter of trust and distrust indicate that the construction we can place upon his particular activities will be generally meaningful, and the narrator's failure to achieve a resolution is thus suggested to be of universal relevance.

The narrator of this novel has an even greater reluctance to commit himself than Ishmael: we never learn the result of the confidence man's dealings with the passengers—whether he cheats or helps them. We never really discover, in other words, how to read the phrase "confidence man." The idea of "trust" is presented satirically, surely, but in two ways; it is both admirable and foolish. The reasoning that the confidence man employs so persuasively, as well as that of the passengers he confronts, is shown to be both sensible and specious, and on occasions the general human use of any sort of analogical reasoning is questioned. The satire throughout the novel, in fact, is so generally and erratically directed—at times against all men, all reasoning, and all constructions upon life—as to display a game without rules and a world beyond understanding. This verbal chaos suggests that any conviction about man's universe—and this includes confirmed skepticism—is a kind of monomania.

In a chapter entitled "Worth the Consideration of Those to Whom It May Prove Worth Considering," the narrator equivocally presents us with what is perhaps the only sort of statement in this novel that is not somewhere flatly contradicted. He remarks that

upon the whole, it might rather be thought, that he, who, in view of its inconsistencies, says of human nature the same that, in view of its contrasts, is said of divine nature, that it is past finding out, thereby evinces a better appreciation of it than he who, by always representing it in a clear light, leaves it to be inferred that he clearly knows all about it.[3]

The rhetorical hesitancy here parallels and parodies the narrator's unwillingness to do anything but present a state of inconsistency that can be said to be neither permanent nor temporary; he will not describe, at the end of the book, what has happened or what will happen. As the multicolored "cosmopolitan," the last incarnation of the confidence man, "kindly" leads an old man away into the darkness, he remarks, "Something further may follow of this Masquerade."

I do not think we can assume here that Melville means he intends to write a sequel, for this remark may be integrated perfectly into the attitude that the narrator displays throughout the book. He consistently refuses to make any statement by which the narrative might be structured in some way. *The Confidence-Man* has no ending, and Melville suggests by this means that the inconclusiveness to which a reader has been exposed can only be sustained.

This novel exhibits a world that is totally without meaning, in which both ambiguous satire and equivocal eulogy are so universally directed as to be aimless. The tone of the narrative is dominantly comic; neither the "ineffable" of *Moby-Dick* nor the "nothingness" of *Pierre* are relevant:

[3]Herman Melville, *The Confidence-Man: His Masquerade,* ed. Elizabeth S. Foster (New York: Hendricks House, 1954), p. 77.

it is simply a matter of extended confusion founded upon the thoroughly tenuous dichotomy of "trust" and "distrust." The narrator's elusiveness is so complete as to present the tensions of the novel in the most purely dramatic terms, as the interactions of many more or less equally significant characters and ways of viewing experience with no resolution whatsoever and no dominant character or perspective. Melville may be said here to have solved the narrative difficulties of the problem of imaginative failure by simply disregarding them. The narrator has disappeared, and although ambiguity can be sustained in this way, *The Confidence-Man* must be read, I suggest, in terms of the more explicitly consequential tensions of *Moby-Dick* and *Pierre* if it is to assume the relevance it seems to deserve. "Nothing remains," says the speaker at the close of the chapter I have mentioned, "but to turn from the comedy of thought to that of action" (79). The confidence man himself is the white whale of the comic chase.

Although it is perhaps most central in "Heart of Darkness," the failure of imagination is a major theme in much of Conrad. Often Conrad presents a narrative and simultaneously demonstrates that to give it a disciplined and final meaning is impossible, suggesting that the fictional world he has created can only be approached by verbal contradictions and a sense of mystery.

Lord Jim provides an excellent example of the manner in which Conrad, through Marlow, suggests that his story is founded upon complete uncertainty. Marlow is never sure that he understands Jim or his problematical moral failure. Throughout the novel, as in "Heart of Darkness," the moral framework of such a failure appears to be both arbitrary and illusory. Marlow implies that all men of imagination are inevitably prone to just such a mistake, that the complexity of their responses to experience may at any time prove too severe to be withstood by any code of morality or honor. A most relevant analogy to Marlow's thought may be found in a passage from *Pierre:*

For there is no faith, and no stoicism, and no philosophy, that a mortal man can possibly evoke, which will stand the final test of a real impassioned onset of Life and Passion upon him. Then all the fair philosophic or Faith-phantoms that he raised from the mist, slide away and disappear as ghosts at cock-crow. For Faith and philosophy are air, but events are brass. Amidst his gray philosophizings, Life breaks upon a man like a morning. (340)

In *Lord Jim,* however, the cause of failure is the imagination itself, and not the "brass" of some sort of unformed, raw experience. It is the complexity and intensity of Jim's awareness of his situation on the "Patna" that is intolerable to him, as it is to Marlow, and that might even be seen to precipitate a temporary insanity. Imaginative complexity causes the loss of imaginative control.

Marlow cannot condemn such a loss, for he sees it as the result of the illusory nature of the codes and meanings by which control is effected. He insists throughout the novel upon the separateness of man and the order he attempts to achieve, a separateness that is dramatically emphasized in Jim's final gesture, an acceptance of destruction that is a self-crucifixion. Jim's cross is the imaginative intensity with which he assumed, in an attempt to satisfy his outraged sense of honor, a moral responsibility. He demands from the world an unambiguous vindication of his moral sense; he cannot assume the conception of meaning and morality as arbitrary illusions unconnected with man that Marlow frequently suggests, but must accept them absolutely and satisfy them with his entire being.

The novel provides no solution. Indeed, Jim's death may be seen as a compliance with the advice that Stein has given Marlow: " 'In the destructive element immerse. . . . That was the way. To follow the dream, and again to follow the dream—and so—*ewig—usque ad finem.*' "[4] Jim follows his "dream" and in doing so comes to an end that is needless and foolish to all save himself. What is most curious about Stein's "destructive element," moreover, is that it is not characterized as something antithetical to or beyond imagination. The "dream" and the "destructive element" are both analogous to the "sea" in Stein's terms, and it thus appears that the imagination is its own negation. This is a striking parallel to Marlow's narrative insistence that imaginative control may be destroyed by imagination itself. The same imaginative seriousness that most values discipline and meaning destroys either the reality of those meanings or him that must adhere to them.

The quality of Conrad's general preoccupation with the disparity between meaning and experience, between man's illusions and an indifferent or chaotic or simply empty world, is easily oversimplified. In my account of "Heart of Darkness," I have remarked the insolubility of Marlow's sense of a nothingness at the center of things with his assertion of the presence of a "darkness": Marlow redefines a flat inability into a metaphorical conflict: man against the dark powers. I have suggested, also, that Conrad may be dramatizing, perhaps somewhat ironically, Marlow's propensity for this sort of imaginative gesture. Conrad's awareness of the fallacy of constructing a scheme by which the

---

[4]Joseph Conrad, *Lord Jim, Works,* IV, 214–15.

self is metaphorically seen in conflict with a supernatural power like "darkness" is unquestionable; he suggests in *Nostromo,* for example, that such a vision of the world is a basic attitude of the "man of action": it is "the obscure superstition of personal fortune from which even the greatest genius amongst men of adventure and action is seldom free."[5]

And yet Conrad's skeptical awareness of this idea of a "personal fortune," in which the universe is placed in direct and significant relation to a man, does not prevent him from adopting the idea itself; we may consider, for example, his description of Decoud's death: "A victim of the disillusioned weariness which is the retribution meted out to intellectual audacity, the brilliant Don Martin Decoud, weighted by the bars of San Tomé silver, disappeared without a trace, swallowed up in the immense indifference of things."[6] In this passage, "retribution" is "meted out"; the universe is concerned with man in a personal and moral way. In the next breath, however, we are presented with "the immense indifference of things." On the one hand, the world is governed by a stable and predictable

[5]Joseph Conrad, *Nostromo, Works,* VIII, 469. I do not consider *Nostromo* except in my somewhat narrow concern with a paradox of attitudes in Conrad. Jocelyn Baines, however, describes the book in a way that is useful for my more general purposes: "...idealism and skepticism, faith and want of faith, both seem to lead to disaster. *Nostromo* is an intensely pessimistic book; it is perhaps the most impressive monument to futility ever created." *Joseph Conrad: A Critical Biography* (New York and London: McGraw-Hill, 1960), p. 310.

[6]*Nostromo,* p. 501. Baines has also remarked that the "audacities" of Decoud and Nostromo are paradoxically "the most constructive actions in the book" and those that have the worst consequences for the actors. His entire discussion of *Nostromo* is important in relation to the idea of imaginative failure. Baines, pp. 310–13.

code that a man can know; on the other hand, it is indifferent, and while this indifference is a manner of defining
things in itself, it is in violent opposition to the idea of
"retribution" and possibly a step toward a recognition of
the complete impenetrability of experience that we have
seen in "Heart of Darkness."

In order to emphasize sufficiently the dimensions of the
disparity in Conrad's own imagination that I have noted,
we may consider *Under Western Eyes*.[7] Like many of the
protagonists of the later novels, Razumov has no tradition
or meaningful heritage behind him; his patronymic is a
fiction, and he can only suspect that he is the bastard son
of a nobleman. He therefore identifies himself with his
country, Russia, and determines to legitimatize this identification by means of his studies and his intellect. His sudden immersion in a revolutionary conspiracy against the
government thus destroys all possible meaning for him, and
this destruction is the dramatic foundation of the novel.[8]

The narrator's treatment of Razumov's story is remarkable in two ways: first, it is clear that this story is a moral
story for him; second, he insists upon his limitations as a
viewer of the experiences that he relates, upon his "Western eyes." Both of these qualities are apparent in the fol-

[7]*Works*, XII.

[8]The intensity of Razumov's passion for a significant identity parallels that of Ahab, Kurtz, Jim, Sutpen, *et al.* Like Sutpen, "disorder"
affects Razumov "profoundly," "unreasonably" (76); his simple confusion becomes a 'destructive horror" (78). His experience, like that of
Kurtz and the others, eludes definition; he "inspires confidence" in
those who know him, and in every case this confidence is disap-
pointed. His confession at the end of the novel, which precipitates
the assault upon him that renders him deaf and crippled, implies
nothing so much as the futility of his final atempt to justify confidence, to assume Natalia Haldin's morality and thus vindicate her
trust. And in this way he is the general counterpart of Lord Jim.

lowing quotation: "...for this is a Russian story for Western ears, which, as I have observed already, are not attuned to certain tones of cynicism and cruelty, of moral negation" (163). At the same time, however, the narrator not only articulates Razumov's struggle with meaninglessness but also suggests that the illusory nature of all human pursuits may be the fundamental premise of his narrative. On one occasion, for example, he speaks of man's "miserable ingenuity in error" and his "short-sighted wisdom" (305). In other words, the narrator characterizes the story as structured around a human inability to order experience, while both declaring that he cannot understand this inability and conceding that the experience of the novel is impenetrable to him.

The speaker's forceful imaginative removal of himself from the world of his story is a characteristic Conradian gesture; I mention it here because I think it may be clearly seen to depend upon the fundamental disparity in Conrad's imagination with which I have been dealing—his ability to present a world without meaning while retaining his hold upon some idea of morality or truth that is unaffected by his inquiring vision. We must remember that it is primarily the "moral negation," the "cynicism," that the narrator of *Under Western Eyes* cannot understand; he dramatizes this negation completely but insists that it is peculiar to the East, to Russia, and irrelevant to himself. In the light of our awareness of Marlow's despair in "Heart of Darkness" and of his refuge in constructing the metaphor of "darkness," the narrator's denial of a connection between himself and the implications of his story is suggestive. The idea of the "Western eyes" of Conrad's narrator is an artificial device—as most readers will feel—a euphemistic metaphor like "darkness" by which the narrator excludes himself from the centerlessness of his story. In the novel this device functions to suggest the impenetrability of the experience of the story and to conflict with the expectations of meaning created by the intelligible movement of the story itself. We feel, in other words, that the narrator will understand the matter in spite of himself. This, again, is the split vision that we have seen must be associated with the presentation of general imaginative failure.

This imaginative paradox, which is so central to Conrad's writing, is revealed explicitly in the preface to *A Personal Record:*

Those who read me know my conviction that the world, the moral world, rests on a few very simple ideas....It rests, notably, among others, on the idea of Fidelity. At a time when nothing which is not revolutionary in some way or other can expect to attract much attention I have not been revolutionary in my writings. The revolutionary spirit is mighty convenient in this, that it frees one from all scruples as regards ideas.[9]

It may be noted that Conrad's very postulation of a moral idea implies not the truth but the necessity of such convictions; he is concerned with the functional nature of something like "Fidelity." His general awareness of the unreality of such convictions, moreover, is expressed only a few paragraphs later. A critic, he says, has remarked that certain excuses that Conrad gave for *The Mirror of the Sea* were "good reasons for not writing at all," and Conrad responds with a statement that seems perfectly understandable in relation to "Heart of Darkness": "I admit that almost anything, anything in the world, would serve as a good reason for not writing at all" (xxiii).

[9]*Works,* IX, xxi.

Among Conrad's later novels, probably the best example of a flat admission of imaginative failure is *Chance,* and although it is a somewhat better novel than Melville's *Pierre,* there are general resemblances between the two. The story, for example, is all Marlow's; the relation of the central characters—Roderick Anthony, De Barral, and Flora—to his narrative preoccupations is usually unsatisfactory and often simply obscure. The quality of this relation is defended, of course, in Marlow's insistence upon his inability to understand the world he describes: "The trouble was that I could not imagine anything about Flora de Barral and the brother of Mrs. Fyne. Or if you like, I could imagine *anything* which comes practically to the same thing."[10] This remark might well serve, certainly, as a definition of the narrative method of Ishmael or of Quentin Compson, and parallel to it are Marlow's continual assertions that he and his major informant, Powell, cannot see beyond "surfaces."

Having established his inability, Marlow then proceeds, characteristically, to suggest that the characters of whom he speaks are themselves examples of the futility of the struggle to order experience. Captain Anthony's pursuit of Flora may be seen as a Sutpen-like attempt to possess something unequivocally and by doing so render it and all experience meaningful. Flora serves simply as a means by which Anthony's rightness and generosity will be expressed. Given his view of Flora as an incarnation of a universal loneliness and centerlessness, Anthony is able, by controlling her, to control the universe; instead of "shaking an indignant fist at the universe," he can simply pat Flora's hand (344). His feeling for Flora is something "more or less

[10]*Works,* XIV, 210.

than love": "Something as incredible as the fulfillment of an amazing and startling dream in which he could take the world in his arms—all the suffering world—not to possess its pathetic fairness but to console and cherish its sorrow" (348). It is clear, however, that for Anthony, perhaps for all, consolation implies possession. His attempt to isolate Flora—along with her father—on his ship seems his way of insuring the absoluteness of both physical and imaginative control.

The images of Flora and her father—like all experience that one attempts to render intelligible—or both enigmatical and hollow. Flora's eyes are like the inscrutable ocean, and yet even to Marlow she is "not so much unreadable as blank" (20). The great De Barral himself, furthermore, is mediocre and empty as well as invincibly obscure; for Marlow he is a perfect example of the general condition of mankind.

The blankness of these characters is complicated, too, and the theme of the struggle for order extended, by the facts that Flora and her father attempt to achieve imaginative control over each other, to transform each other into a microcosm in which their relation to the universe will be defined. Their attempts are frustrated by Anthony's uncompromising efforts, which are dramatized in his taking them aboard his ship—an act that is for him, of course, a moral act—and thus creating the situation that reveals the basic tensions of the novel.

But these tensions are resolved, and in a curious manner. De Barral becomes evil, a potential murderer, and dies; Flora confesses her "love" for Anthony; they live happily upon the sea and at the mercy of "chance" until the captain dies in a collision. Later, Flora has her memories, which are suggested to be both simply romantic—like Marlow's nostalgia for the sea—and totally obscure. This conclusion has the effect, I think, of emphasizing the weaknesses of the novel, the arbitrary nature of the characters themselves: De Barral is both empty and evil; Anthony's paralysis at crucial moments arises from both dullness and sensitivity; and Flora herself seems both tragically mysterious and intolerably silly.

Like the characters of *Pierre,* although to a lesser degree, the characters of *Chance* appear insufficient as figurative expressions of the centerlessness of human experience. The separation between narrator and character, which—like the ambiguities of the characters themselves—is itself the supposed evidence of this centerlessness, serves mainly to emphasize the insufficiency. The insistence upon disorder or confusion is too great, and the struggle for order that was apparent even in *Under Western Eyes* is unreal. Everyone, including Marlow, has given up. The unequivocal assertion of the failure of imaginative control—as in *Pierre* —deprives the failure of meaning.

I shall confine my discussion, in this chapter, of Faulkner's work to an analysis of *The Sound and the Fury,* and my reasons for doing so are these. Although structural disorder in Faulkner is not always concomitant with an explicit preoccupation with the failure of imagination, such disorder is always indicative in Faulkner of certain assumptions about language and meaning that I shall discuss in my concluding remarks. Because this general disorder always implies, as I see it, a single view of language, it is unnecessary here to proceed through various novels and stories, remarking, for example, that structural disorder seems explicitly parallel with the inadequacy of language in *As I Lay Dying* whereas in *Light in August* such disorder seems to be presented with little clarifying emphasis upon the separateness of words and experience. That such structural disorder is, in fact, the dominant quality of Faulkner's writing, furthermore, has been shown—and, I think, thoroughly and conclusively—by Walter J. Slatoff.[11] Slatoff traces the phenomena of unresolved ambiguities, incomplete patterns and approximate significances through the major fiction, and he leaves no doubt of the consistency and single-mindedness of Faulkner's deliberate preoccupation with structural confusion. His conclusion is to see this preoccupation as a "quest for failure," a quest which may have the effect of suggesting the greatness of what has been attempted but too often simply emphasizes the inconclusiveness and self-obfuscation of the attempt itself. My own concern, of course, is to examine this dual effect of Faulkner's persistent structurelessness in terms of its linguistic characteristics and consequences. It may be simply noted at this point that since the emphasis on general disorder in Faulkner has been recognized, there remains the matter of establishing more detailed relations between the particular use of language I have described and the various works that I have not considered.

"Each in its ordered place."[12] With this last phrase of *The Sound and the Fury* we realize that the idiot Benjy's "order"—the difference between his placid and empty satisfaction and his total, bellowing despair—depends upon the permanence of a simple spatial movement from "left to right" as he rides to and from the cemetery. Faulkner suggests consistently in this novel, however, that all the

[11]*Quest for Failure: A Study of William Faulkner* (Ithaca: Cornell University Press, 1960).

[12]William Faulkner, *The Sound and the Fury* (New York: Random House, Inc., 1946), p. 336.

attempts at imaginative control that the story contains are equivalent to the order created in the mind of an idiot. To Benjy's mind the world takes the form of a small number of catchwords, the principal of which is "Caddy" or, as the men in his pasture-turned-golf-course say, "caddie." The presence of Caddy, his sister, gives Benjy his greatest stability and security; the awareness of her absence—constantly re-emphasized for Benjy by her "symbolic" presence in the word "caddie"—triggers the inarticulate moaning that seems the essence of profound chaos.

The same tendency to build a world around exclusive "symbols" may be seen in Jason Compson IV, whom Faulkner has called "the first sane Compson since before Culloden" (Appendix, 16). Jason exhibits his "sanity," we may suppose, in his pragmatic vision, in his avowed reluctance to meddle—which may seem a recognition of the invincible and confused separateness of persons and of experiences—and in his particular lack of moral scruples and his general unwillingness to take any human rule or totem seriously. And yet the meaning that Jason sees in his existence—that which justifies his losses to the "New York Jews," the tedium of his life at the store, and his continual and frantic financial juggling—depends upon a symbolic view that is as specious as Benjy's own: "Of his niece he did not think at all, nor the arbitrary value of the money. Neither of them had had entity or individuality for him in ten years; together they merely symbolized the job in the bank of which he had been deprived before he ever got it" (321). Jason's concern with his niece and the money, as well as with Quentin his brother and Caddy, is concentrated in his feeling of deprivation and his fanatical belief that this deprivation is in fact the metaphor by which his identity is established: he is the eternal loser, sufferer, and under-dog.

It is not only the emptiness of Benjy's or Jason's imaginative order, however, that is apparent in this novel. The vision of resurrected religious truth that moves Dilsey so deeply, as an example of the sort of "truth" with which Faulkner presents us, is the standard product of a theatrical specialist in such visions, the monkeylike preacher with the great voice, Shegog, the power of whose speech is directly proportional to its incoherency. The entire Easter framework of the story, moreover, is conspicuously hollow and ironical—in which Jason crucifies himself by transforming his particular losses into the eternal metaphor of the righteous, sacrificial loser and Benjy is suggested by the Easter chronology to be harrowing hell.

The most penetrating account in the novel of the struggle for order, however, lies outside the Easter mythology, in Quentin's account of the day of his suicide, and it exhibits his attempt to detach himself from all such struggle. Quentin's "confession" to his father of incest with Caddy is received by Mr. Compson as a futile attempt to render experience meaningful; Quentin recalls the conversation as follows:

...and i i wasnt lying i wasnt lying and he you wanted to sublimate a piece of natural human folly into a horror and then exorcise it with truth and i it was to isolate her out of the loud world...and he and now this other you are not lying now either but you are still blind to what is in yourself to that part of general truth the sequence of natural events and their causes which shadows every mans brow even benjys you are not thinking of finitude you are contemplating an apotheosis in which a temporary state of mind will become symmetrical above the flesh and aware both of itself and of the flesh it will not quite discard you will not even be dead and i temporary.... (195–196)

Quentin's father celebrates the "finitude" of existence, of course, the mortal "sequence of natural events," by drinking himself to death, but his pronouncements have crucial effect. Quentin comes to understand that his desire for incestuous consummation is merely an attempt to deny the nature of the confusions of experience as "temporary" states of mind; it is an attempt to establish order by means of transforming momentary "folly" into eternal "sin."

It is not because of incestuous desire, in other words, that Quentin commits suicide, nor is it because of Caddy's aborted marriage—to pay for which, along with Quentin's year at Harvard, Benjy's pasture was sold—but because he has been deprived of any way in which he might see the desire and the marriage, as well as the suffering of his brother, his sister, and himself, in a meaningful perspective. He has become aware through his father that his attempt to transform the temporal complexity of his experience into an "apotheosis"—as I infer, into an eternal and significant order—is as empty as experience itself, is itself an example of mortal futility and confusion. The result of this awareness—of a recognition and acceptance of the meaninglessness of human experience—is his suicide: "It's not when you realise that nothing can help you—religion, pride, anything—it's when you realise that you dont need any aid" (99).

This novel does not simply provide us with an excellent example of Faulkner's concern with imaginative failure, but defines that failure in terms that are different from any that we have previously encountered. Quentin's striving for coherent meaning is consistently equated with his concern with time, and not only in the fact that his attempt to make his experience meaningful is inseparable from destroying its temporariness. His search for order is an attempt at the eternal, certainly, but it is interesting to note that the search itself—in its endless, mechanical, and inescapable persistence—is associated with time and clocks. Quentin's father describes this association as "that constant speculation regarding the position of mechanical hands on an arbitrary dial which is a symptom of mind-functioning" (96). But for Quentin such "speculation" has become not simply the "symptom" but the symbol of consciousness— the consciousness that he will relinquish. His destruction of his father's watch and his flight away from the bells and whistles that mark time are simply metaphorical pre-enactments of his suicide. The arbitrary measurement of time has become representative, we may suppose, of the arbitrary but ceaseless function of the mind itself, of the emptiness of the order that the mind continually must strive to create. Because Quentin is aware of this arbitrariness, he can conquer time—like consciousness—not by an act of ultimate and immutable vision but only by an act of relinquishment.

CHAPTER VII

Conclusion
The Instability of Metaphor

THE problem of imagination that I have described might of course be considered as a matter of specific influences and as a matter to be approached by the explanations in traditional cause and effect of literary history. There is no doubt of the influence of Melville and Conrad upon Faulkner. Faulkner has stated that *Moby-Dick* was a book that he read once a year and that it might be the greatest work of American fiction because of the magnitude of its failure.[1] He has further expressed his particular interest in "Heart

---

[1] "Q. Why do you give *Moby-Dick* the top position? A. Well, I don't. I'm just naming ones that might be: I wouldn't give it the top position, but if I did, it would be for the reason that I rate Wolfe higher than Hemingway, that *Huckleberry Finn* is a complete [*sic*] controlled effort and *Moby-Dick* was still an attempt that didn't quite come off, it was bigger than one human being could do." Frederick L. Gwynn and Joseph L. Blotner, eds. *Faulkner in the University* (Charlottesville: University of Virginia Press, 1959), p. 15. My attention was first drawn to Faulkner's specific references to Melville—and to Conrad—by Richard P. Adams' "The Apprenticeship of William Faulkner," *Tulane Studies in English*, Vol. XII (1962), 113–156.

of Darkness," and one need only turn to "The Old People"
or "The Bear" to see obvious parallels in the treatment, for
example, of the idea of wilderness.[2] And although there is
apparently no scholarly evidence that Conrad read Melville, it would seem extremely unlikely that he did not
do so.[3]

The seriousness with which we ought to consider these
specific but vague "influences," however, is qualified by
the complex implications of the imaginative attitude that
I have discussed. Even if the beginnings of this attitude
might be tentatively located, for instance, in the novel—
and for this purpose we might consider the somewhat special cases of *Tristram Shandy* or *Wuthering Heights*—the
attitude itself remains a problem of large and vague dimensions. Its dominant characteristic is an intense self-consciousness toward language and imaginative order, with a
growing awareness of the complex artifices of imagination
and of the drastic limitations that must arise from an
attempt to structure these complexities. Even if this basic

[2]"Q. Sir, what are some of your favorite books? A. *Don Quixote*,
some of Conrad, *Heart of Darkness*, *The Nigger of the 'Narcissus.'...*" Gwynn and Blotner, p. 61. The interest in *Don Quixote*
seems characteristic of writers concerned with imaginative failure,
and undestandably so. Conrad says of Cervantes' knight: "He rides
forth, his head encircled by a halo—the patron saint of all lives
spoiled or saved by the irresistible grace of imagination." *A Personal
Record, Works,* IX, 37.

[3]Jocelyn Baines's suggestions on this are ambiguous. At one point
he describes a correspondence between Melville's *Redburn* and Conrad's *Nigger* as "almost certainly a coincidence," while a few pages
later he notes that "perhaps Conrad had also been reading Melville at
the time." *Joseph Conrad: A Critical Biography,* p. 77n, p. 80n. James
Baird declares that it is a "recorded fact" that Conrad read Melville,
but as to where this fact is recorded Baird is silent, and I have been
unable to find it. *Ishmael* (Baltimore: Johns Hopkins Press, 1956),
p. 125.

characteristic were all, it would seem beyond the scope of the ascribing of specific influences and beyond the present concerns of literary history. But it is not all, and the discovery and description of an apparently special and curious attitude toward language is at most an introduction, and possibly a misleading introduction, to the problem. In the following discussion I shall try to show that the problem of imagination I have considered here may be seen to result not from a special perspective but simply from a deliberate insistence upon a view of language fundamental to literature and to thought. My purpose is to attempt to define this view of language more thoroughly, and in that way to suggest the possibilities for further inquiry.

To this point in my discussion I have emphasized the chaotic and nihilistic effects that a concern with imaginative failure may have; I have done so largely because from "Heart of Darkness" onward the emphasis is upon failure, upon the kind of moral and ideological deprivation that may arise from an awareness of the limitations of imaginative structure. Such a treatment of the problem, however, inevitably slights its stylistic implications and fails to recognize not only the kind of "meaning" that is inseparable from the presentation of sustained verbal complexity but also the conception of the function of metaphor implicit in an awareness of probable failure. The matter of "failure" is ambiguous, and it suggests a particular sort of stylistic attempt. This is especially apparent, we have seen, in *Moby-Dick,* and it may be helpful to return to that book for a moment in order to secure the basis for a more general discussion of this matter of style.

I have remarked that Ishmael communicates in both a positive and a negative way. Because he is convinced that no single vocabulary can capture what is most important about the experience he considers, he is able to employ in his narrative all the vocabularies of which he is aware: the world of his narrative is composed of many perspectives, from the "scientific" to the "supernatural," all of which are present on a kind of sufferance. One of the effects of such a narrative technique, as I have suggested earlier, is to transform the world of the narrative into a fantasy world, where particular entities and meanings are powerful because vague, intense because unrealized. The quality of this world as fantasy, furthermore, may be defined not simply as the effect of the specific "supernatural" languages that Ishmael employs but as the effect of the mixture of language that he presents; the world of *Moby-Dick* is fantastic because it is kaleidoscopic, because it includes and sustains tensions between many possible kinds of language, because it seems to contain all language and all meaning.

We may recall, too, the importance of the "potential" that is created in *Moby-Dick* and that I have suggested to be characteristic of the narratives of "Heart of Darkness" and *Absalom, Absalom!* This potential is created because nothing is ever communicated unequivocally, because no consistent, single vocabulary can ever be established as the most significant. Its power and suggestiveness arise from our expectations that it will be at last resolved in an ordered way, that the tensions among disparate vocabularies are only temporary, that they will finally be shown to be consistent in terms of a great whole. And the very fact that the anticipated resolution does not occur may serve to reinforce a reader's feeling of the reality of some immense idea that is being indirectly presented. When the potential is not realized, in other words, the illusion of meaning nonetheless remains, for the multiple and unresolved possibilities become—because they are unresolved—

157

the supposed evidence of some unspeakable and immense consistency: they are evidence of the inexpressible, the image of something that is the greatest possible meaning because it is not meaning at all. We thus find the darkness illuminating.

Throughout my discussion I have insisted upon this effect and described it some detail; the question that remains is *why*. Why should a reader respond to verbal contradiction and complexity with a feeling that the inexpressible has been communicated? Why does the expectation of meaning, which seems necessary to this sort of response, often continue to exist in spite of the fact that such complexity is sustained? And why, finally, should a writer present language that seems antithetical to the traditional moral and imaginative certainties of fiction? Once again I would like to postpone more direct consideration of the matter for a moment, as the answers to these questions may be suggested by examining a work in which the use of language is parallel to the novels I have described, but in which the emphasis upon moral failure and complete confusion is not so great as it is in "Heart of Darkness" or *Absalom, Absalom!*: Faulkner's "The Bear."

In the general outlines of the major portion of its narrative, "The Bear" seems a neat parallel to *Moby-Dick* and "Heart of Darkness." The hunt in general is suggested to be an attempt to give order to something that may be finally beyond order, the wilderness and the quintessence of the wilderness, the bear. In order even to see the bear, however, Ike McCaslin finds it necessary to put aside his gun, his compass, and his watch, to relinquish, in fact, the very idea of a hunt or of any search with implications of ultimate resolution. Gun, compass, and watch, it may be noted, all seem representative of ways of rendering experience intelligible, and it would thus appear that in order to know the bear Ike must give up all the means of such intelligibility at his command.

This idea is reinforced by the fact that upon every occasion when Old Ben is encountered or brought to bay, the basic terms of the encounter always reflect the absence of the simplest sort of order. The first example, of course, is the necessity of Ike's losing himself in the woods before he can confront the bear. Later, when Ike and Sam Fathers bay Old Ben, they do so with a "fyce," a seemingly insignificant mongrel whose shrill courage is indistinguishable from folly. Lion himself, the dog who is essential to the killing of the bear, is as inscrutable in his power as Old Ben; he is a part of the wilderness, lending himself—on a kind of sufferance—to men. Boon Hogganbeck, finally, is incoherency personified. He has never been known to hit anything with his gun, he has the body of a brute and the mind of a child, and he accomplishes the death of the bear by entering into a chaotic, knife-to-claw struggle with it that is another sort of nullification of the rules of the hunt, of its dignity and restraint.

The character in whom the possibilities of response to the idea of "wilderness" are most articulated, again, is Ike himself. Ike looks, but he does not shoot; he refuses to resolve the hunt, which may be seen as a tension between order and disorder, and his refusal, as we learn later, has something to do with "truth." On the one hand, Ike's refusal is just that, a deliberate gesture and thus a kind of controlled uncontrol; on the other hand, it is somehow not deliberate but simply an inability to act or to consummate. The refusal and the inability, furthermore, appear inseparable It may be that one must refuse to kill Old Ben just because once killed he is only a dead bear, because he loses all the vague significance of the wilderness, just as the wilderness itself is slowly being plotted and destroyed. It may be also that what is involved is the kind of fantastic paradox that we find in "The Old People," in which Walter Ewell, who never misses with his rifle, shoots at the great deer, the "grandfather," and hits a spike-horned yearling. In "The Old People" the ineffable spirit of the wilderness exists—the deer leaves tracks, for example—but it continues to be real only if one does not attempt to apprehend it in a final way: the capturing or the killing can have the effect only of anticlimax and unsatisfaction. There is this flavor of anticlimax about the death of Old Ben in "The Bear," but there is also another suggested consequence of the attempt to apprehend the "reality" of the wilderness.

When Ike returns to the wilderness for the last time he finds Boon—and this passage seems one of the most powerful in all American literature—sitting at the base of the huge Gum Tree:

...the whole tree had become one green malestrom of mad leaves, while from time to time, singly or in twos and threes, squirrels would dart down the trunk then whirl without stopping and rush back up again as though sucked violently back by the vacuum of their fellows' frenzied vortex. Then he saw Boon, sitting, his back against the trunk, his head bent, hammering furiously at something on his lap. What he hammered with was the barrel of his dismembered gun, what he hammered at was the breech of it. The rest of his gun lay scattered about him in a half-dozen pieces while he bent over the piece on his lap his scarlet and streaming walnut face, hammering the disjointed barrel against the gun-breech with the frantic abandon of a madman. He didn't even look up to see who it was. Still hammering, he merely shouted back at the boy in a hoarse strangled voice:

"Get out of here! Dont touch them! Dont touch a one of them! They're mine!"[4]

Faulkner has glossed this passage for us; he tells us that Boon is trying to *repair* his gun, in which a shell has jammed, and that he doesn't want anyone to shoot the squirrels until he can.[5] But there appears here, in distinct contrast to this idea of repairing, a decided emphasis upon fanatical destruction of the gun, and it cannot be doubted that, whether repairing or destroying his gun and consequently the idea of the hunt, Boon is at the moment completely insane. As the killer of Old Ben, it may be that he now possesses the mystery, that he has apprehended the reality of the wilderness, and his passion of ownership can now take the form only of an intense and futile confusion.

It thus appears in "The Bear" that the only possible approach to the wilderness, the reality or the "truth" of it, is Ike's method; this is the only alternative to anticlimax or to madness. The fundamental idea of this approach that is not an approach is, again, the maintaining of imaginative distance, the refusal to bring to issue or to resolve, and an insistence upon one's lack of imaginative control. As an imaginative attitude, it is characterized by McCaslin Edmonds' reference to Keats' "Ode on a Grecian Urn": " 'She cannot fade, though thou hast not thy bliss,' McCaslin said: 'Forever wilt thou love, and she be fair.' "[6]

---

[4]William Faulkner, "The Bear," *Go Down Moses* (New York: Random House, Inc., 1942), p. 331.

[5]A glance through the pages of any of the interviews with Faulkner often reveals either his penchant for drastically oversimplifying what he has written or his apparently deliberate invocation of the obscure. Both gestures are fast becoming notorious, as, for example, is his Nobel Prize speech taken in conjunction with the despair and disorder of the fiction, particularly the earlier fiction.

[6]In *Go Down Moses*, p. 297. I have often remarked this sort of

And it is here that one of the primary ambiguities of "The Bear" and most of Faulkner's writing becomes apparent: this ambiguity lies in the motivation of the "suspension" that I have described. Insofar as Ike's motives for relinquishing his patrimony are similar to those for his adopting a suspended attitude wherever "truth" becomes an issue, a reader has the feeling that there is no mystery here at all. The land has a curse on it, we are told, a curse of slavery and miscegenation and incest, and the pursuit of "truth" cannot be successful or even attempted until the curse has ended. The failure to order, in other words, springs from a conviction that a certain kind of order exists, and it is not a failure at all, but a condition of the "hell" in which we live and which some day may become "heaven," or at least Eden, again. There is no way of doing away with this problem in Faulkner, I think, but it is possible to suggest that his moral conviction of a curse may be frequently subsumed under a more general conviction of a basic quality of language and imagination, and whether this quality is seen by him to be the result of a curse or the fall of man or anything else is secondary to the pervasive effects and less fabulous assumptions of the quality itself.

For a reader cannot fail to notice the parallels between

---

sustained unresolution or suspension of imaginative progress, but it is worthwhile to note the form it takes in McCaslin's mind. The image of withholding sexual consummation or of attempting it unsuccessfully, with its concomitant tension between man-words as orderer and women-life-void as that to be ordered or informed is implicit in all the works I have considered at length, and not only as the basic metaphor of penetration. Note, for example, Marlow's conception of the jungle as Woman, his contemptuous awe of Flora de Barral in *Chance,* or Sutpen's crucial difficulties with women, or Pierre's.

the manner in which Ike McCaslin approaches the "truth" of the wilderness and the usual form of Faulkner's own rhetorical methods. The insistence upon incoherency, upon the abrogation of rules, and upon permanent unresolution as positive values that have been seen to be characteristic of Faulkner's imagination are all expressed metaphorically in Ike's attitudes. The very suspension of pursuit upon which Ike relies, in fact, as well as his reliance upon losing his way, is the dramatic equivalent to Faulkner's use of verbal suspensions, the long and seemingly directionless sentences that never come to issue.[7] If we follow this parallel to its logical conclusion, we may establish the proposition that "truth" depends somehow upon this sort of suspension; it depends upon what we might normally assume to be the antithesis of truth—upon the refusal and inability to structure experience or, in the language of my discussion, to create a metaphor. Why this should be so, however, is a more complicated question.

The dramatic parallel with "The Bear" cannot help us here, for in that story the idea that success means failure is

[7]Faulkner has said of the idea of the hunt: "The hunt was simply a symbol of pursuit. Most of anyone's life is a pursuit of something. That is, the only alternative to life is immobility, which is death. . . . And always to learn something, to learn something of—not only to pursue but to overtake and then to have the compassion not to destroy, to catch, to touch, and then let go because then tomorrow you can pursue again. If you destroy it. . .then it's gone, it's finished. . . The pursuit is the thing, not the reward, not the gain." Gwynn and Blotner, pp. 271–72. Compare this with my remarks about Ishmael's attitude—that it is "only the seeking that can be known"—and with Walter J. Slatoff's remarks about Faulkner: "If the absolutely crucial thing is to go on trying—if it is the act of trying which gives man his immortality and which even, as Judith Sutpen suggests, makes life matter and gives it meaning—then one canot really risk success, and failure becomes a kind of success." *Quest for Failure,* p. 261.

expressed metaphorically in the death of the bear and the dissolution of the wilderness, and we would prefer a more literal explanation. The metaphors that we take from this story, however, are understandable to a point. It seems clear that the idea of the hunt is a way of expressing the attempt to create order, and that the successful resolution of the hunt should therefore be somehow analogous to the creation of meaning, and yet this very creation, again, has implications only of failure. Once the meaning is achieved and the metaphor composed, then the power of it—the value that one had in mind—is lost.

The "power" or "value" of any given metaphor, then, if the analogy holds, is not only a function of the capacity of such a metaphor to order or to reduce the complexities and disparities of imaginative experience. It seems also to depend upon the fact that a metaphor somehow reproduces these complexities and disparities, and that the force of a metaphor entails our feeling that disparate implications and perceptions are there held in suspension, contained but not contained, reflecting a movement toward a meaning that—in terms of the manner in which the parts of the figure strain against each other—seems beyond words. I. A. Richards has noted the importance of this sort of "action" in metaphor:

We must not, with the 18th Century, suppose that the interactions of tenor and vehicle are to be confined to their resemblances. There is disparity action too. . . . Thus, talk about the identification or fusion that a metaphor effects is nearly always misleading and pernicious. In general, there are very few metaphors in which disparities between tenor and vehicle are not as much operative as the similarities.[8]

[8]*The Philosophy of Rhetoric* (New York: Oxford University Press, 1936), p. 127. Compare also a remark by Colin Murray Turbayne: ". . . a good metaphor, like a good portrait, does not hold a mirror up

The Instability of Metaphor

Unfortunately, Richards does little more than note this "disparity action," yet his remark is provocative.

It seems clear that it is the "disparity action" of metaphor that is most relevant to the concerns that I have been pursuing. What it involves is this: when two disparate systems of implications—which may be only single words—are brought together in a juxtaposition where meaning is intended or expected, the ordinary conventions of usage are upset, and we tend to associate this strained relation with synthesis or with ultimate coherency, with the "similarity" that the metaphor is presumably working toward. The next step in the process is a sort of "filtering" action: the terms of the metaphor interact so as to suppress some implications of each term and emphasize those implications that may be seen to be properties of both terms.[9]

---

to the face of nature but vividly illustrates some features of it and neglects others. It is probably a better metaphor even if there are some differences which may throw into relief the startling likenesses." *The Myth of Metaphor* (New Haven and London: Yale University Press, 1962), p. 214.

[9] I have generally assumed that we take for granted the idea that a metaphor structures experience, but for a careful demonstration of the way in which even the simplest sort of metaphor begins to organize our view of experience, see Max Black, *Models and Metaphors* (Ithaca: Cornell University Press, 1962). Black remarks (pp. 44–45) that a metaphorical interaction between two " things" or "systems of thing" acts as a "filter" that "selects, emphasizes, suppresses or organizes features of the principal subject by implying statements about it that normally apply to the subsidiary subject." I would extend this argument and say that the process of "filtering," which I have discussed as the process of "reducing," works upon both terms of the metaphor, that "principal" and "subsidiary" are not as meaningful as Black seems to imply. This is really only my insistence on adopting more thoroughly the "interactional" view of metaphor that he presents. On pp. 236–37, Black defines the view of metaphor as imaginative order that I am suggesting: "A memorable metaphor has the power to bring separate domains into cognitive and emotional

The Limits of Metaphor

The moment, however, that the similarity becomes clear, and the relation between the terms becomes stable, then the sense of disparity dwindles. For the stability between vocabularies or attitudes that were discrete—and our ability to understand fully the verbal relation in which these conflicting attitudes are contained—depends upon their not remaining discrete, upon the reduction of the complexity that was so suggestive and so powerful, and thus upon the dissolution of the disparity that made the meta-

---

relations by using language directly appropriate to one as a lens for seeing the other [I would add "and vice-versa" here].... The extended meanings that result, the relations between initially disparate realms created, can neither be antecedently predicted nor subsequently paraphrased in prose."

Black also suggests (p. 41) that one of the terms of a metaphor may be a system of "current commonplaces" or stock implications. This, I think, is the notion of the "root metaphor," under which we try to subsume unstructured experience; a reader may find this expansively pursued in Stephen C. Pepper, *World Hypotheses: A Study in Evidence* (Berkeley and Los Angeles: University of California Press, 1961). The root metaphor situation occurs in Melville, Conrad, and Faulkner, of course, but I think its presentation can be better understood in terms of the more ideally primitive situation of composing metaphor out of complete disorder that these writers most often emphasize. What the root metaphor situation demonstrates in terms of the failure of imagination are the limitations of the root metaphor, its exclusiveness, rigidity, artificiality, and so on. The root metaphor implies, also, that a promising start in the creation of order has been made, that one set of implications is more important than most others. This is something that Melville, Conrad, and Faulkner are seldom willing to admit except to show, as is occasionally the case, that the most important metaphorical system fails.

Finally, a remark of Kenneth Burke's is relevant to the idea of the "reducing" action of metaphor: "The various systematized theories as to just what important relationships and situations there are, particularly in the social and political realm, confront one another as competing orators, hence requiring either dialectical compromise or dialectical resolution by reduction to an ultimate order." *A Rhetoric of Motives* (New York: Prentice-Hall, 1950), pp. 206–07.

phor so effective.[10] The very metaphorical unity that is
the ostensible object of the imaginative struggle destroys
the reality and the meaning of that struggle—the struggle
that is exhibited in the initial strain and conflict between
the terms of the verbal relation—and destroys the meaning
of the metaphor itself, for the moment that the disparate
elements become ordered and unified, then the imaginative
force of their synthesis is lost.[11]

It would seem, then, that the imagination may fail in
two ways. In the first place, it may be impossible for a
character or narrator—given the complexity and diversity
of his imaginative experience—to accomplish the metaphorical fusion that I have described: this is the failure
with which I have been concerned throughout this discussion. In the second place, it now appears that this sort of
"failure" is justified to some extent by another possible
kind of imaginative collapse. If the potential unity of a
given metaphor were to be pursued, if one attempted to
define this unity, then the order established by the metaphor would cease to have meaning. The manner in which
this dissolution of meaning may come about, however, is
more complicated than I have suggested.

The supposed fusion that a metaphor can achieve may
not be a fusion at all. By insisting upon the similarity between the terms of a given metaphor—between two previously disparate sets of implications—a third set of impli-

[10]A "third vocabulary," of course, will have been formed by the
stable interaction of the first two. Of this I shall say more later.

[11]Cf. Turbayne, *Myth of Metaphor*, p. 21: "The attitude shifts
produced by an effective metaphor point to a later stage in its life.
A story often told—like advertising and propaganda—comes to be
believed more seriously. Those details stressed tend to stay stressed
while those suppressed tend to stay suppressed until another effective
metaphor restores them."

cations is created. This third vocabulary is, of course, a kind of category, which subsumes like aspects of the two vocabularies with which one began. It is not, however, a metaphor; it does not structure the initial elements into a whole, but only provides a way of talking about them that is separable from them. That is to say, this new vocabulary may classify the vocabularies with which we began, but the movement of the imagination in this case is expansive and additive rather than reductive and unifying.[12] The similarity of the elements of a metaphor can result in the creation of another kind of language, but this language merely takes its place among those with which we began; the new

[12]Cf. William Empson: "...the two ideas compared here do not illuminate one another...they produce a third more general idea which reduces them to the status of examples of illustrations. The metaphor as such is destroyed...." *The Structure of Complex Words* (Norfolk [Conn.]: New Directions, n.d.), p. 347. This paradox, by which the metaphor can only achieve resolution by destroying its effectiveness as metaphor, is implied by Philip Wheelwright: "In unifying the heterogeneous elements presented to it as raw materials for cognition the mind *may* act as Kant supposes it to do: viz., it may unify in such a way that the radical heterogeneity of the raw materials is virtually nullified in the process. The result then is a conceptual one—we see the world as rationally ordered, in terms of causes and effects, substances and attributes, measureable space and time or space-time, necessities and probabilities, and so on. But the synthesis which expresses our actual living encounter with the world—the 'vitalistic' synthesis—tends to preserve the heterogeneous in its natural character (i.e. in its heterogeneity), thereby giving it a place in a meaningful whole that is not mechanical but vital. Our world thus contains an irrepressible element of paradox, of dramatic tension, and of unresolved ambiguity." *The Burning Fountain: A Study in the Language of Symbolism* (Bloomington: Indiana University Press, 1954), p. 96. The "vitalistic synthesis" that Wheelwright mentions is not, of course, a "synthesis" in the sense of resolution or reduction, but simply of juxtaposition. In the case of any "synthesis" for the purpose of cognition and order, probably he would accept Kant's supposition.

system is relegated to its place among the previous systems, and the complexity of imaginative perception is increased rather than decreased.

Ernst Cassirer summarizes nicely the imaginative situation that I have in mind here, although he sees it as a matter of alternatives:

Logical contemplation always has to be directed toward the *extension* of concepts; classical syllogistic logic is nothing but a system of rules for combining, subsuming and superimposing concepts. But the conceptions embodied in language and myth must be taken not in extension, but in intension; not quantitatively, but qualitatively. Quantity is reduced to a purely casual property, a relatively immaterial and unimportant aspect. Two logical concepts, subsumed under the next-higher category, as their *genus proximum,* retain their distinctive characters despite the relationship into which they have been brought. In mythico-linguistic thought, however, exactly the opposite tendency prevails. Here we find in operation a law which might actually be called the law of the leveling and extinction of specific differences. Every part of a whole is the whole itself; every specimen is equivalent to the entire species. The part does not merely represent the whole, or the specimen its class; they are identical with the totality to which they belong; not merely as mediating aids to reflective thought, but as genuine presences which actually contain the power, significance, and efficacy of the whole.[13]

I have suggested that "mythico-linguistic" thought—supposing that it is analogous to my idea of metaphor—cannot be pursued, that if it is it tends always to resolve itself into "logical contemplation." That is to say that one ends as he began, that the mechanical, additive, and dead significances of systematic thought are the only sort of significances pos-

[13]*Language and Myth,* trans. Susanne K. Langer ([New York]: Dover, 1946), pp. 91–92.

sible, and that the organic and vital pseudosignificances of the metaphorical imagination—the expectations of meanings beyond words—can neither be satisfied nor sustained.

There are, in short, finally no alternatives here at all. Any actual, stable "unity" created out of metaphor can only be an insistence upon the similarities of its elements. The disparities of these elements, the disparities upon which the supposed structural value of the metaphor rests, must be excluded from such a unity.[14] The expectation

[14]Martin Foss, in describing the metaphorical tension implicit in the idea of prayer, characterizes this "unity" nicely: "The mystic has described his experience, now and then, as an identification with God. But in doing this he has reduced the metaphorical process of prayer to a symbolic relation of identity. It is this identification which has often been called the very nature of mysticism. But, in fact, this identification is rather a breaking away from the dynamic and truly mystical process of prayer. It is a rational endeavor to transform the metaphorical tension of prayer, which is neither identity or difference, into an absolute and pure identity. The result of this rational transformation, therefore, had to be the hypostasis of a purely abstract concept of reason...." *Symbol and Metaphor in Human Experience* (Princeton: Princeton University Press, 1949), pp. 80–81. This book is worthy of much more notice than it has received. Foss is not specifically concerned with imaginative failure, for he does not consider at any length the connection between the metaphorical tension and process and the rational or "symbolic" reduction that is, as I see it, both inevitable and fatal in a given metaphor. But he does place the emphasis in his discussion of metaphor where it belongs—upon the tension of the metaphor, its quality as process and potential, and upon the idea that "symbolic" reduction is a refutation of metaphor. My idea of the worth of this book is not proportional to the number of times that I cite it. I read it only late in the process of composing my own arguments, and had I read it earlier, I might have used it as the focus or even the basis of my own discussion of metaphor. I have refrained, at this point, from incorporating it more thoroughly into this discussion because I feel that my contentions—as well as Foss's—will seem of more value if made independently. Foss's book, again, must be read by anyone who is interested in the function of metaphor and of imagination itself.

of a consistent structure greater than this disappointingly exclusive unity—an expectation that the metaphor excites—cannot be satisfied by pursuing the metaphor to resolution. Metaphor creates the expectation, in other words, of a unity *of* differences, but the pursuit of this expectation results only in a unity *and* differences. The metaphor seems to contend that its disparities are part of a great whole, but no amount of concentration upon the metaphor can express this "whole." The creation of the "third vocabulary" that I have mentioned does not, again, express it. It apparently depends upon remaining unverbalized and unrational, and while we may accept this condition, we can neither explain nor really know—in the stable and consistent manner of rational language—the nature of the "order" of which we seem to be aware.

A corollary to this line of thought may be the idea that "meaning" depends upon a vitalistic tension between order and disorder, between unity and multiplicity. But as neat as this proposition seems, it is essentially problematic. The metaphorical balance and tension between unity and disunity is so problematic, in fact, that it becomes both illogical and dangerous to assume, as we often do, that the two sorts of imaginative failure that I have mentioned—the ends of which are either nonsignificant multiplicity or nonsignificant unity—are simply aberrations, that Ishmael and Ahab, for example, are representative of two sorts of insanity. In this view—and I think it is a superficial one—the idea that a metaphorical order may become so unambiguous as to destroy the very conception of structure and meaning might be—and has been—seen as the result of a mistake. We might say, for example, that the reduction of imaginative complexity to imaginative consistency is due to a misguided conception of the nature of metaphor itself, that the postulation of such consistency is only one of the functions of metaphor. A "true" metaphor, we might say, is always provisional, always explicit regarding the fictional quality of the verbal fusion that it seems to be working toward; it emphasizes the separateness of its elements as much or more than the connectedness of them.[15]

It is just this problem, I think, that the novelists that I have considered have tried to solve by their characteristic insistence upon the disparity of the elements of a possible metaphor and upon the permanence of this disparity. They employ a type of "metaphor" that, if we say that metaphor implies the creation of order, is not metaphor at all. The simile and the oxymoron both function to insist upon the separateness of elements that—in part because they are coupled grammatically—seem the elements of a potential synthesis. The fact that the simile is extended may sustain an illusion of ultimate meaningfulness while insisting upon the great dimensions—given the multiple disparities it contains—of such a meaning. This is the "unity of differences" that we observe in *Moby-Dick* and that I have called the "ineffable."[16]

But this unity, the idea of "whiteness," is not, of course, a unity at all. The rich imaginative complexity that I have described in Melville, Conrad, and Faulkner is only "consistent" in the sense that it is forced together, contained by

[15]Turbayne holds that this "true" metaphor, which, I think, is achieved in an extended way only by means of the simile and related figures, always displays its metaphorical quality and its complexity explicitly. Hereafter when I say "true" or "ideal" metaphor, I shall refer to the "metaphor" created in the simile.

[16]The idea of an "ineffable" is thus inherent in the idea of metaphor itself, as I shall show at greater length later. For a brief discussion of the manner in which the oxymoron in particular is allied with "mysticism" and may be used to express the ineffable, see Kenneth Burke, *A Rhetoric of Motives*, pp. 324–28.

a narrator or narrative, and in the sense that the very existence of complexity—of the bringing together of many disparate sets of implications or kinds of discourse—will be apprehended by the mind of a reader as the indication that a stable "metaphor" is being constructed, that the foundations of an imaginative order are being established. Once again we may see the importance of expectations. The writers with whom I have dealt rely upon a reader's feeling that meaning will be achieved in a kind of unity or consistency, and they go to great lengths to reinforce this feeling. The multiple, strained verbal relations within a narrative are accompanied with the emphatic assertion that all disparities will be resolved, whether this assertion takes the form of a character such as Ahab, of Marlow's moral consciousness, or of the overt struggle for identity and significance in Quentin Compson.

It is the reality of the expectation of some ultimate unity or order, in other words, that makes the complexity of imaginative perception and the disparity within a given metaphor so suggestive, and this expectation lies at the heart both of the function of a metaphor and of the motives for metaphor. The idea of the ordering value of metaphor, asserted always by Ahab and often by Marlow and Quentin, is not the result of a mistaken view of metaphor; it is simply an assertion of the expectations that a metaphor suggests and, most important, upon which it relies as a metaphor.

If we say that Ahab and those like him are insane, or that they attempt to make the world a part of the self, or that they "take metaphors literally"—if we suggest that their view is simply a mistake, then we ignore the fact that their attitudes represent a necessary ingredient in the metaphorical complex, that such characters are only the dramatizations of the expectation of unified structure implicit in the very idea of metaphor.

Opposed to this expectation is the attitude of Ishmael, of half of Marlow's and Quentin's minds, and of Ike Mc-Caslin. Here an insistence upon the ordering or cognitive function of metaphor is seen to be fundamentally destructive—destructive, I suggest, in the ways that I have described. As these characters see the matter, we must always be aware of the provisional quality of all metaphor, of the complexity and disparity that such provisional metaphor expresses; we must be aware, in other words, that the expectation of order or unity cannot be satisfied. This conception of the imaginative problem, as we have seen, is ultimately just as destructive as the attitude of Ahab, for it results in the kind of confusion that we encounter in *Absalom, Absalom!*

What is involved here is a contradiction at the foundations of the metaphorical process. If the expectation of order is pursued, meaning will be destroyed; it may thus be said to depend upon not resolving a metaphorical tension, upon the expectation of ultimate consistency remaining unsatisfied. And yet the more one insists upon the unreality of this expectation, then the more one emphasizes the confused aspect of the supposedly metaphorical relation. When the function of metaphor is shown to depend upon an expectation that is false, the idea of metaphor dissolves.

This paradox within the idea of metaphor is dealt with successfully in *Moby-Dick;* Melville renders the expectation of a final resolution thoroughly ambiguous throughout the narrative, but this expectation becomes definitely unreal only at the last. In this way he makes full use of this expectation as a stylistic device, and, even though its complete artificiality is finally apparent, it has served its purpose. The ramifications of Melville's achievement, however, are startling, for it would seem to indicate that metaphor is only a matter of art, of expression, of suggestive embellishment, that its ordering or unifying or cognitive function is an illusion of art, and that to pursue this function or to depend upon it can only reveal that it is nonsensical. But this cognitive function of metaphor is the essence of imaginative perception; we must assume that meaning can be achieved by the construction of stable relations among the complexities of imaginative experience; we must rely upon metaphor as a structural device, as the structural device. And yet what Melville, Conrad, and Faulkner—among others—continually demonstrate is that such reliance cannot be sustained if we are to preserve the illusion of meaning itself.[17]

[17]Walter J. Slatoff sums up this ambivalence in Faulkner as follows: "It cannot have meaning and yet it must. The statement does not simply describe a dual perspective (sometimes seems to matter, sometimes not) or an uncertainty (may or may not matter) or even a paradox (does and does not matter). The simultaneous 'cant' and 'must' suggests a desperately divided and tormented perspective, a condition of mind which tries to move simultaneously and intensely toward both order and chaos and which understandably seizes upon the figure which most nearly moves in both directions, the oxymoron." *Quest for Failure*, p. 251. And Charles Feidelson suggests that the problem of any "symbolist" author must be that of treading a line between clear and mechanistic order and unified and organic chaos: "At the same time every attempt to grapple once more with rational multiplicity can only lead the symbolist back to his starting point. It is the divisiveness of logic that occasions his effort to live in the unitive world of language. In practice the symbolist will be caught between the consequences and the necessity of his method— between a sort of pathless void, pregnant with significance and a radically unknowable world of absolute distinctions." *Symbolism and American Literature* (Chicago: University of Chicago Press, 1953), p. 71.

The Limits of Metaphor

The cognitive function of metaphor must be denied if we are to place any value in art and thought, and yet this function cannot be denied for the same reason. And even to be aware of this paradox is to lose faith in the illusion of meaning that art, and thought, can create and upon which the mind depends. It has been suggested that the solution to the problem lies in constructing "true metaphor," the provisional metaphor that always displays the qualified nature of the potential synthesis, the sort of metaphor that I have called the simile. The remedy, this argument holds, is "as if" thinking.[18] Such an argument, however, pretends to an impossibility: it pretends that metaphorical structure can be thoroughly provisional and still maintain its structural implications—that our expectations of order, of the cognitive value of metaphor, can be consistently denied and yet continue to exist as one of the necessary ingredients of meaning. It pretends, then, that the cognitive value of metaphor can still be taken seriously even though every attempt to realize this value serves to call it into question, even though its very existence depends upon its unreality.

The imaginative problem that I have described—to summarize and expand briefly—arises from the metaphorical paradox, in which cognitive expectations must exist in a sustained tension with their antithesis, the disparate implications and imaginative complexity that renders these

[18]I shall deal at length with the supposed desirability and possible satisfactions of "as if" thinking later; for the moment it may be said that this condition of qualified but intense acceptance is just the condition that Faulkner attempts to create by emphasizing the instability of his "myths." The cognitive value of such an attitude, as one look at "Heart of Darkness" makes clear, is much more tenuous than some writers have suggested.

expectations meaningful. We might, in an attempt to solve the problem, elevate the "artistic" or "expressive" function of metaphor over the "ordering" or "cognitive" function, since "artistic" or "expressive" metaphor is always provisional, always powerfully suggestive of the imaginative struggle itself. And yet to attempt this is to ignore the contradiction at the heart of the matter, to forget that this "artistic" function always implies the "cognitive" function, that it is the cognitive expectation that renders the expressive complexity so suggestive and so "meaningful." The artistic function of metaphor, in short, depends upon the ordering function, which is to say that it always implies its own dissolution, and that imagination depends upon its own failure.

We may now understand more completely the significance of what I have called the "ineffable," for this awareness of a reality beyond language—as I have remarked—relies upon the illusion of order out of disorder and unity from disparity that is the basic property of the metaphor itself. The expectations that act upon verbal complexity to suggest an ineffable reality are the cognitive expectations that are created and refuted by any "true" or provisional metaphor, any metaphor in which the disparity of the verbal elements is sustained. The ambiguity between order and disorder that such metaphor exhibits is the basic source of any sense of the "ineffable."[19] The disappearance

[19]Foss discusses the "potentiality" of the metaphorical relation in a most suggestive manner in regard to the "ineffable." The "contingency" he remarks is the coincidence of the elements of a metaphorical juxtaposition, the "necessity" is similar to the "expectations" of my own argument, and Foss's "process" is of course the metaphorical process as a whole: "Potentiality, as the category of life and consciousness, is never merely contingent, as the possibility of things is, but assumes necessity in the process in which it is involved. In

of the ineffable, furthermore, results inevitably from pursuing one's supposed ability to know it. And the consequent denial of this ability to know—a denial of cognitive powers with a proportional insistence upon imaginative complexity for its own sake and not as a means to an ineffable end—is of course the general parallel to the dissolution of metaphor itself.

The expectations that are so necessary in transforming verbal complexity and confusion into an awareness of great "meaning" are tenacious, but they cannot endure the persistent disappointment to which they must be subjected if the reductive, simplifying force of the composed or resolved imaginative consistency is to be avoided. The illusion of coherency cannot be preserved when coherency is pursued, and yet to fail to pursue it is finally to assert

---

this process the necessary meaning lies permanently ahead of the potential consciousness as its direction and future.... The potential realizes an actuality which, in spite of being not yet, nevertheless somehow *is* already. This, indeed, is the secret of life and consciousness that the potential is in a mysterious tension and unity with a never-ceasing actuality; that the communion of present and future is a consciousnes which always is present, but always has to realize itself in a future. This inner articulation of the actual and potential, of present and future, is an awareness, not of a detached object but of its own direction and development." *Symbol and Metaphor,* pp. 73–74). Foss, again, does not really analyze what happens when this "future" is pursued, but he seems to understand that it must not be pursued if the metaphor is to retain its effectiveness as such: "Only tendency is what we call 'general' or 'universal,' because only tendency stretches beyond a multitude of predicates. The universal is the tendency of expansion, *it anticipates as tendency its predicative fulfillments, which can only be conceived in the process of propositional thinking*" (p. 19, my italics). These "predicative fulfillments" are, I think, the ultimate reductions to which a metaphor may be taken and which destroy its quality as metaphor. It should thus be clear that Foss is describing an ideally metaphorical situation here, in which such "fulfillments" are as yet unrealized explicitly.

the confusion of imaginative perception for its own sake: the suggestive force of this confusion—the possibility of the ineffable—becomes nothing at all.

The problem is nicely defined, in somewhat different terms, by George Marion O'Donnell in an essay that reveals, as I see it, the most fruitful approach to Faulkner's art: "... the moment a tradition begins to be formalized into a code, it commences to lose vitality; when it is entirely formalized, it is dead—it becomes pseudo-tradition."[20] This argument is parallel to my own, and its similarities may be roughly exhibited if we substitute "metaphor" for "tradition." The point at which a metaphor becomes "formalized," at which the disparity between the terms of any single metaphor becomes so slight as to deprive that figure of its force, is clearly what is involved here; this is the phenomenon that we recognize, probably, in what we call a "dead metaphor" or when we say that a given phrase is "no longer metaphorical."[21] Again, however, we may note that

[20]"Faulkner's Mythology," in *William Faulkner: Three Decades of Criticism,* ed. Frederick J. Hoffman and Olga W. Vickery (East Lansing: Michigan State University Press, 1960), p. 85. While noting this as a narrative problem, O'Donnell applies it successfully to the characters of various novels.

[21]Turbayne summarizes this process as follows: "There are three main stages in the life of a metaphor. At first a word's use is simply inappropriate. This is because it gives the thing a name that belongs to something else. It is a case of mis-using words... and, therefore, of breaking the conventions. All the great sort-crossers were unconventional. Great metaphors are no better or no worse off in this regard than the ordinary mistakes in naming.... Our first response is to deny the metaphor and affirm the literal truth....

"But because such affirmation and denial produce the required duality of meaning, the effective metaphor quickly enters the second stage of its life; the once inappropriate name becomes a metaphor. It has its moment of triumph. We accept the metaphor by acquiescing in the make believe.... The metaphor is used by us with awareness to illuminate obscure or previously hidden facts.

the deadness of metaphor is scarcely a problem for Melville, Conrad, and Faulkner except in the sense that this deadness is always avoided and with such drastic results. If characters such as Ahab are continually working toward "formalization" within a given narrative, that narrative is always straining away from such unequivocal structure toward complexity and toward confusion.

It has frequently been remarked, also, that Faulkner attempts to create "myth," and in connection with my discussion to this point the myth involves not simply a formalized structure of immense proportions but a structure that is expressed by its disparity, complexity, inexplicability, and its vitality. Florence Leaver has described "myth" in connection with Faulkner in a similar manner:

Primitive or literary, myth is created by, and in turn creates, a sense of wonder, a sense of the marvelous. Neutralization of nature has no place in myth; it is the enemy of wonder and of the sublime. . . . Earth in this myth is never neutral; it may be unfriendly, and even its fecundity is 'violent,' but man is always aware of its eternal progression of growth and death and growth again.[22]

I think that if we widen the range of this remark, we shall be able to understand fully the kind of illusion created by Faulkner and by Melville and Conrad when they are at their best, the kind of illusion that they are attempting to create constantly.

"The moments of inappropriateness and triumph are short compared to the infinitely long period when the metaphor is accepted as commonplace. . . . Within this long period the original metaphor may develop in various ways only one of which is a case of taking metaphor literally." (*Myth of Metaphor,* pp. 24–25).

[22]"Faulkner: The Word as Principle and Power," in *Three Decades,* p. 205. O'Donnell also mentions Faulkner's mythic quality in connection with the struggle not to formalize myth into "dead myth" or "allegory." In *Three Decades,* p. 8.

The Instability of Metaphor

The reluctance to "neutralize nature" may serve as an analogy. If we substitute for "natural complexity" here *verbal* or *imaginative* complexity, we discover that the reluctance to neutralize becomes the reluctance to impose order upon imaginative complexity by the construction of the sort of stable metaphor that I have mentioned. And like "nature," the general imaginative content of myth and metaphor, their verbal complexity, is fecund and sugges tive, and its interrelations "violent."

The analogy with "nature" is also useful in another way. We may now understand why the use of language that I have described is initially associated—in *Moby-Dick* and "Heart of Darkness," and in "The Bear"—with uncivilized contexts, with the sea or the wilderness. For sea or wilderness function to prevent the structural neutralization that I have remarked; order may be easily seen to be particularly artificial and generally unsatisfying when applied to experience that is assumed to be wild and new, and at the same time, of course, this very newness may seem to imply the promise of some ultimate order beyond order. The idea of a wilderness, I would suggest, is simply an allegori zation of the complexity and of the expectations of unity implicit in imaginative perception, with the difference that in this situation the expectations of a final order seem a part of the situation itself, and thus may be more easily sustained.

In the natural situation it is least difficult to suggest by means of the artificiality of language some nonlinguistic reality, even though it must become apparent—as in *Moby-Dick* at the last—that the complexity that one confronts is not natural but, like all complexity, imaginative, and that the possibilities of final structure are only the limited possibilities of language itself. Like all else about the presentation of this imaginative problem, the illusion of the non-verbal—the intense expectation of a "reality" that a natural situation suggests—even in a successful myth like *Moby-Dick,* is not durable, but it is nonetheless important to note the manner in which it has been created.

The important ingredient in the "natural situation," moreover, if it is to provide a sense of the nonverbal or the more than verbal, is not that it is natural but simply that it is new, for with a new situation the illusion of the nonverbal may be at least initially established. If the situation can be suggested to be unstructured in some essential way, then the artificiality of the perspectives one brings to it may imply a potential reality, rather than—as in *Absalom, Absalom!*—a complexity that is merely verbal, only a confusion of linguistic artifice.

Here another analogy between the idea of wilderness and the ineffable and the idea of metaphor and the ineffable becomes important. I have suggested that the wilderness situation has two essential implicatons: first, it implies that the verbal structures that one brings to bear upon it are artificial; second, it implies an expectation of discovery, or an expectation that some nonverbal reality will be apprehended. It seems clear, also, that each of these implications depends upon the other, or perhaps that they are the same: perhaps our awareness of the artificiality of language implies the expected realization of the nonverbal.

The connection with the idea of metaphor itself is now most apparent. For when two vocabularies or sets of implications are juxtaposed in a relation that either intentionally or circumstantially promises "meaning"—and this would include all relations save the few that might be presented specifically as "unmeaningful"—our attention is immediately drawn to the artificiality of these vocabularies, or to their mutual inadequacy as effective and sufficient structures. It is this awareness of the artificiality or inadequacy of the terms of the metaphor that implies not only a potential reality beyond these terms in particular but also a reality *beyond the artificial in general,* a reality beyond language. The expectation of an nonverbal "meaning," in other words, springs from the insufficiency of the separate elements of the metaphor, which is suggested simply by the juxtaposition itself, by the fact that there are two terms, two sets of implications, and not one.[23]

The metaphor relies, then, upon the inadequacy of its elements for a statement of its movement toward something greater than these elements, and yet the essential magnitude of this "something greater" depends crucially

[23]Cf. Foss, *Symbol and Metaphor,* p. 60: "The metaphorical process of speech does not enhance the kind of generality which is systematic, i.e. which is an addition of parts to a whole. It is the unique generality of the intentional process to which the terms are sacrificed, and it is their mutual destruction in this process out of which a new and strange insight arises. . . . In blasting the symbols and shattering their *customary meaning* the dynamic process of the searching, striving, penetrating mind takes the lead and restores the truth of its predominant importance" [my italics]. The idea that a metaphor destroys the significance of the elements of which it is composed has been dispensed with by some philosophers and critics, who thus undervalue Foss's contribution to our knowledge of the function of metaphor. W. K. Wimsatt, for example, suggests that the words fused into a metaphorical structure, such as a poem, have their new value only by retaining their old value. (See W. K. Wimsatt, Jr., and Monroe C. Beardsley, "Symbol and Metaphor," *The Verbal Icon* ([Lexington]: University of Kentucky Press, [1954])). No one, I think, would seriously contend otherwise. If we set out to understand the idea of metaphor, however, rather than to fix on what seems unfruitful in Foss's expression of it, we may conclude that this passage points, although somewhat extravagantly, to a drastic change in the *status* of the values of a metaphor's terms as the metaphor takes effect, a change, perhaps, of the sort that I am proposing here.

upon the integrity of these same elements, upon the real force of their conjunction. Each term of a metaphor, in short, must exhibit in itself opposed qualities of artificiality and reality, weakness and strength. These terms must both maintain their integrity and relinquish it; they must be both ends and means. This is the critical instability of metaphorical language.

Moby-Dick is an excellent example of this instability. There the possible vocabularies are many, and Ishmael devotes himself to most of them with significant imaginative intensity. Our response to his narrative takes the double form of a confused apprehension of many separate realities and an expectant apprehension—expectant partly because of Ahab—of various temporary artifices that look forward to some final inexpressible reality. These artifices, however, can never be vindicated by a larger reality. At the same time, the expectation of this reality can never, in the course of the novel, be flatly denied, for if each vocabulary that Ishmael employs were to maintain what I have called its "integrity," then we would be confronted not with complexity but with confusion. The resulting, insistent exclusiveness of each vocabulary would render each not simply artificial but artificial and directionless. And this is the sort of artifice that was to be alleviated, the sort of artifice with which the narrative and the process began.

Out of a dissatisfaction with the structuring powers of imagination and in the conviction that to be content with the composed artifices of imagination is to accept failure as success, the writers that I have considered here employ a multiplicity of linguistic perspectives and use the extended simile and the repeated oxymoron to enforce the disparities among these perspectives, to sustain the strains

and tensions that, together with the intense expectation
that order will be achieved, suggest a meaning beyond
words. The simile and the oxymoron—with all other figures that work to the same purpose—are representative of
these writers' insistence upon a certain kind of metaphor,
a metaphor that never loses its complexity and vitality, in
which the suggestion of order is maintained only because
it is nearly lost in the richness of the imaginative experience which the metaphor presents. And this, after all, is
the ideal or "true" metaphor.

To accomplish this, however, is to insist more and more
upon the unreality of the ordering or cognitive function
of metaphor, and as this function dwindles the richness of
experience approaches the confusion of experience. We
have seen in *Moby-Dick* that it is possible for Melville to
sustain the illusion of cognitive expectations through a
stylistic achievement, but that this involves his never taking this expectation seriously. In Conrad and Faulkner
these expectations are desperately serious; a character or
narrator may rely upon them for the moral significance
of his life, and when this illusion of possible order is pursued it breaks down all the more quickly.

The general consequence of this process would seem to
be that the function of metaphor becomes more and more
artistic, a kind of game in which one may indulge only on
an illusory basis. This is not to say that metaphor can no
longer aid us in making sense of life, but that the terms of
the relation between metaphor and life are wholly altered.
We may indulge in metaphorical thought exactly in the
way that we indulge in art; in both cases we must recognize that the assumption that art and thought are meaningful depends upon their quality as fictions, as provisional
metaphors or similes. The expectations that make art or

thought significant have become explicitly illusory, and the only factors upon which we may rely, I think, are our own capacities either to forget the unreality of these expectations—which any moment of self-awareness makes apparent —or to change the game, to recreate the expectation of order continually by adopting a different set of metaphors, and thus to re-establish our ability to respond to the frequently unintelligible incantations and confusions of art and life with optimistic anticipation. It is this quality of forgetful and unaccountably resilient optimism—given the absence of any real expectations of order or any final intelligibility—upon which a writer such as Faulkner, inevitably, I think, has come to rely so heavily.

Again the matter of "as if" thinking becomes relevant, for it is just this optimism, this infinite capacity for make-believe. that is so often praised or accepted by modern writers of all sorts and disciplines as the solace and retreat of imagination. This is the attitude displayed in the following quotation from Turbayne's *The Myth of Metaphor:*

The third course is to be fully aware of the presence of the disguise; aware that there are no proper sorts into which the facts must be allocated, but only better pictures or better metaphors; and also aware that to adopt a metaphor as metaphor is to alter one's attitude to the facts; and then to treat the language metaphor as a myth, "a myth not to be taken literally, but to be dwelt on till the charm of it touches one deeply—so deeply that when the 'initiated' say 'it is not true', one is able to answer by acting *as if* it were true."[24]

[24]*Op. cit.*, p. 217. Max Black may be seen to recognize the tenuousness of this "as if" attitude: "In *as if* thinking there is a willing suspension of ontological unbelief, and the price paid is absence of explanatory power. Here we might speak of the use of models as *heuristic fictions.* In risking existential statements, however, we reap the advantages of an explanation but are exposed to the dangers of self-deceptions by myths." (*Models and Metaphors,* p. 228).

The Instability of Metaphor

The nature of metaphor itself, I think, calls this idea of a "better metaphor" into question; metaphorical thought must be continually replenished not by "better" metaphors but simply by other metaphors. And it is the dissolution of expectations—a dissolution inevitably yielded by the pursuit of any metaphor—that is always most important in necessitating a change.

The essential hollowness of this "as if" thinking, of this process of continually and self-hypnotically reconstructing the illusion of order, is nowhere more clearly dramatized than in "Heart of Darkness" in particular and in the works of Melville, Conrad, and Faulkner in general. The capacity of such provisional metaphor to structure experience is shown here to be essentially artistic and, I think, essentially frivolous. It is not something upon which—when necessity requires—one can depend.

But here, as Melville would say, we are groping in the "very pelvis of the world," and while it is perhaps inevitable and even suitable that a discussion of certain works of literature should proceed toward its close by noting the effects of those works upon our conceptions of art and life, it is nonetheless a relief to return to the works themselves. It may be said that in *Moby-Dick* Melville discovered more than even he, at the time, was aware. For this novel may be considered the prototype of those works of prose fiction that are concerned with the problem of imaginative failure and the uses of language that, as we have seen, the "failure" entails. *Moby-Dick* must be given this position even though it does not fully express the severe consequences of such failure, or rather, even though Melville may be said to insist that in this failure lies the possibility of greatest success.

For the twentieth-century novelist, however, the dissatisfaction with language that Melville employs in *Moby-Dick* as the means of suggesting some inexpressible meaning becomes the very evidence of the centerlessness of experience. It appears that we have come to expect more of language than language can provide and that our awareness of language as artifice is incompatible with our reliance upon language for purposes of order or—as for Marlow himself —of morality.

Whatever the causes, the process itself may be described. The vague and powerful significances of Faulkner's work depend upon an expectation that—as one reads novel after novel—becomes more and more tenuous: the expectation of success in the continual attempt to unify the disparities of imaginative perception. By this method the myth can never die—it can never become so formalized as to be meaningless—but the price of this questionable vitality lies in the fact that the myth can never really be born into any sort of stability, that it constantly threatens to collapse and does collapse into the imaginative chaos from which it arose. The attempt to create order has become—and, again, the nature of "true" metaphor makes this inevitable—too insistent upon its futility; the expectations that rendered the inconsistencies of Melville's narrative so suggestive and the failure that Conrad exhibits so crucial have disappeared.

It is perhaps unnecessary to add here that Melville's achievement in *Moby-Dick* could not remain, even for Melville, simply an achievement of style or artistic technique—an incredibly successful exercise in "as if" thinking. The despair that we encounter in "Heart of Darkness" pervades the narrative of *Pierre,* with the difference that this despair is never realized with any dramatic power

—never realized because, I suggest, what was once the "ineffable" for Melville had become nothing at all.[25]

The general use of language that is associated with a problematic view of metaphor and imagination, then— and it is the most ambitious not only of the techniques of prose fiction but also of all literature—is not durable. What begins as an achievement of style in Melville, Conrad, and Faulkner soon reveals itself, in each case, as the end of that style. The significance of a concern with imaginative failure depends, impossibly, upon the fact that such a failure never becomes unambiguous; it depends upon a reader's—and a writer's—paradoxical conviction that linguistic disorder, of which the true metaphor is an example, is evidence of the existence of a meaning greater than words, that the intensity of imaginative complexity and conflict only indicates the magnitude of the implied and supposedly ultimate synthesis. When the reality of this inexpressible synthesis is shown, however, to depend upon the unreality of order itself, upon the fact that significant resolution can never take place, then the possibility of metaphor dissolves. The only reality becomes the unreality, the confusions with which one began.

[25]I see *Pierre,* of course, as Melville's explicit recognition of the implications—which I have described—of the ending of *Moby-Dick.*

List of Works Cited

Adams, Richard P. "The Apprenticeship of William Faulkner," *Tulane Studies in English.* XII (1962). 113–156.

Adams, Robert M. *Strains of Discord: Studies in Literary Openness.* Ithaca: Cornell University Press, 1958.

———. *Surface and Symbol: The Consistency of James Joyce's Ulysses.* New York: Oxford University Press, 1962.

Baines, Jocelyn. *Joseph Conrad: A Critical Biography.* New York and London: McGraw-Hill, 1962.

Baird, James. *Ishmael.* Baltimore: Johns Hopkins Press, 1956.

Bezanson, Walter E. "Moby-Dick: Work of Art." In *Moby-Dick Centennial Essays.* Ed. Tyrus Hillway and Luther S. Mansfield. Dallas: Southern Methodist University Press, 1953.

Black, Max. *Models and Metaphors.* Ithaca: Cornell University Press, 1962.

Booth, Wayne C. *The Rhetoric of Fiction.* Chicago: University of Chicago Press, 1961.

Burke, Kenneth. *The Philosophy of Literary Form.* New York: Random House, Inc., 1957.

———. *A Rhetoric of Motives.* New York: Prentice-Hall, 1950.

Cassirer, Ernst. *Language and Myth,* trans. Susanne K. Langer. [New York]: Dover Publications, 1946.

Chase, Richard. *Herman Melville: A Critical Study.* New York: Macmillan Co., 1949.

List of Works Cited

Conrad, Joseph. *The Works of Joseph Conrad*. 20 vols. London and Edinburgh: John Grant, 1925.

Empson, William. *The Structure of Complex Words*. Norfolk [Conn.]: New Directions, n. d.

Faulkner, William. *Absalom, Absalom!* New York: Random House, Inc., 1951.

—————. *Go Down Moses*. New York: Random House, Inc., 1942.

—————. *The Sound and the Fury*. New York: Random House, Inc., 1946.

Feidelson, Charles, Jr. *Symbolism and American Literature*. Chicago: University of Chicago Press, 1953.

Foss, Martin. *Symbol and Metaphor in Human Experience*. Princeton: Princeton University Press, 1949.

Guerard, Albert J. *Conrad the Novelist*. Cambridge [Mass.]: Harvard University Press, 1958.

Gwynn, Frederick L., and Joseph L. Blotner. Eds. *Faulkner in the University*. Charlottesville: University of Virginia Press, 1959.

Leaver, Florence. "Faulkner: The Word as Principle and Power." In *William Faulkner: Three Decades of Criticism*. Ed. Frederick J. Hoffman and Olga W. Vickery. East Lansing: Michigan State University Press, 1960.

Leavis, F. R. *The Great Tradition*. Garden City, N.Y.: Doubleday & Co., 1954.

Melville, Herman. *Moby-Dick or, The Whale*. Ed. Alfred Kazin. Boston: Houghton Mifflin Co., 1956.

—————. *Pierre or, The Ambiguities*. Ed. Henry A. Murray. New York: Hendricks House, 1949.

—————. *The Confidence-Man: His Masquerade*. Ed. Elizabeth S. Foster. New York: Hendricks House, 1954.

O'Donnel, George Marion. "Faulkner's Mythology." In *William Faulkner: Three Decades of Criticism*. Ed. Frederick J. Hoffman and Olga W. Vickery. East Lansing: Michigan State University Press, 1960.

List of Works Cited

Pepper, Stephen C. *World Hypotheses: A Study in Evidence.* Berkeley and Los Angeles: University of California Press, 1961.

Poirier, Richard. "Strange Gods in Jefferson, Mississippi." In *William Faulkner: Two Decades of Criticism.* Ed. Frederick J. Hoffman and Olga W. Vickery. East Lansing: Michigan State College Press, 1951.

Richards, I. A. *The Philosophy of Rhetoric.* New York: Oxford University Press, 1936.

Slatoff, Walter J. *Quest for Failure: A Study of William Faulkner.* Ithaca: Cornell University Press, 1960.

Turbayne, Colin Murray. *The Myth of Metaphor.* New Haven and London: Yale University Press, 1962.

Wheelwright, Philip. *The Burning Fountain: A Study in the Language of Symbolism.* Bloomington: Indiana University Press, 1954.

Wimsatt, W. K., and Monroe C. Beardsley. *The Verbal Icon.* [Lexington]: University of Kentucky Press, [1954].

Index

Absalom, Absalom!, 69–108
  anonymous narrator of, 97, 103
  darkness in, 92
  narrative as simile, 103
  narrative form of, 101
  narrative progression in, 80
  as puzzle, 69
  rhetoric of, 2
  silence in, 98
  success and failure of, 107
  vision of narrators in, 98, 106
  see also Compson, Quentin, *and*
    Sutpen, Thomas
Adams, Richard P., 154*n*
Adams, Robert M., 123, 123*n*
Ahab, 30–45
  ambiguity of his position, 110
  compared to Ishmael, 30, 35, 37,
    40, 43
  compared to Kurtz, 65, 67
  compared to Marlow, 64, 68
  compared to Prometheus, 41, 45
  compared to Sutpen, 82, 85, 95,
    103
  death of, 42, 44
  doctrine of masks, 33
  Melville's ambivalence toward,
    110
  vision versus revenge in, 41
Allusion, technique of in *Moby-
    Dick*, 17; see also *Moby-Dick*,
    narrative technique of

"As if" thinking, 129, 176, 176*n*, 186,
  186*n*

Baines, Jocelyn, 142*n*, 155*n*
Beardsley, Monroe C., 183*n*
Bezanson, Walter E., 39*n*
Black, Max, 165*n*, 186*n*
Blackness, 82, 89
Booth, Wayne C., 131*n*
Burke, Kenneth, 135*n*, 166*n*, 172*n*

Cassirer, Ernst, 169
Chase, Richard, 39*n*
Coldfield, Rosa, 72–75
Compson, General, 92
Compson, Jason III, 70–72
Compson, Quentin:
  compared to other narrators of
    Absalom, Absalom!, 80
  compared to Sutpen, 100
  failure of, 96, 99, 101
  narrative of, 75–81, 96–102
  vision of, 76, 78, 97
Conrad, Joseph:
  ambivalence of vision, 142
  Chance, 146–148
  Lord Jim, 139–141
  The Mirror of the Sea, 145
  narrator's remove from narrative
    in, 144
  The Nigger of the "Narcissus,"
    155*n*

193

Conrad, Joseph *(cont.)*
  Nostromo, 142
  A Personal Record, 145, 155n
  reading of Melville, 155, 155n
  Under Western Eyes, 143–145
  see also "Heart of Darkness"

Darkness:
  in *Absalom, Absalom!,* 92
  as Marlow's metaphor, 67
  opposed to emptiness or nothing-
    ness, 65, 66, 113, 141
Don Quixote, 155n

Empson, William, 168n

Failure of imagination, *see* Imagi-
    native failure
Faulkner, William:
  As I Lay Dying, 148
  "The Bear," 155, 158–163
  compared to Rosa Coldfield, 108
  on the idea of the hunt, 163n
  imaginative failure in, 107
  interviews with, 161n
  Light in August, 148
  on *Moby-Dick,* 154, 154n
  mythology of, 126, 176n
  "The Old People," 155, 160
  rhetoric of, characteristic, 126n
  rhetorical methods dramatized in
    "The Bear," 163
  The Sound and the Fury, 148–153
  see also *Absalom, Absalom!*
Feidelson, Charles, 175n
Figurative language, vague, in
    Moby-Dick, 22
Ford, Ford Madox, 121n, 125, 126n
Forster, E. M., 121n
Foss, Martin, 170n, 177n, 183n

Guerard, Albert J., 65n

Hardy, Thomas, 133
"Heart of Darkness," 46–68
  basic metaphor of, 58, 62, 63, 67,
    116
  compared to *Moby-Dick,* 62
  compared to *Pierre,* 135, 188
  divergences from *Moby-Dick,* 63
  evil as energy and vacancy in, 65n
  failure of language in, 59
  Faulkner's attitude toward, 155n

  "the horror," 47, 61, 66; *see also*
    Kurtz, "the horror"
  ineffable as failure, 115
  ineffable versus emptiness, 66
  meanings of title, 46, 67
  reality in, 55, 59, 60; *see also* Mar-
    low, reality for
  rhetoric of, 2
  see also Darkness, Kurtz, *and*
    Marlow

Imaginative failure:
  destructive aspects of, 126–131
  effects upon narrative technique,
    127
  Faulkner's conception of, 107, 127
  as function of polarities in nar-
    rative, 109
  relation to literary history, 154
  relation to literary influences, 155
  as sexual metaphor, 161n
  split vision of, 110, 128, 145
  structural possibilities of, 121
  validity of, 130
Imaginative instability in the novel,
    1
Ineffable:
  communication of, 3
  versus emptiness in "Heart of
    Darkness," 66
  as failure in "Heart of Darkness,"
    115
  in Ishmael's narrative method, 29
  metaphor, 172n, 177, 177n
  as narrative problem, 120
  paradox of, 114
  progression through *Moby-Dick,*
    "Heart of Darkness," *and*
    Absalom, Absalom!, 106
  simile, 172
  wilderness, 181
Ishmael:
  ambivalence toward Ahab, 37
  atheism of, 39
  compared to Ahab, 30, 35, 37, 40,
    43
  compared to Kurtz, 67
  compared to Marlow, 63, 68
  compared to narrator of *Pierre,*
    134
  compared to narrator of *The
    Confidence-Man,* 137
  narrative method of, 29, 36

Index

Joyce, James, 122, 123n, 126

Keats, John, 161

Kurtz:
compared to Ahab, 65, 67
compared to Ishmael, 67
failure as achievement, 50
history of, 47
as hollow man, 49
"the horror," 61, 65; see also "Heart of Darkness," "the horror"
as "remarkable man," 54
vision of, 54, 61, 61n, 65
voice of, 48

Language:
conception of in *Moby-Dick*, 28
special languages in *Moby-Dick*, 15
usual assumptions about, 7
Lawrence, D. H., 121n, 123–125
Sons and Lovers, 124
Women in Love, 125
Leaver, Florence, 180
Leavis, F. R., 5

Marlow:
compared to Ahab, 64, 68
compared to Ishmael, 63, 68
darkness for, 67; see also Darkness
divided attitude of, 112
inconclusiveness of, 47
moral imagination of, 64, 112
narrative method of, 57
reality for, 52, 58, 60
reliability of, 61n
restraint of, 52
surfaces, 57
truth for, 52
vision of, 114
Melville, Herman:
ambivalence toward Ahab, 110
The Confidence-Man, 136–139
Conrad's reading of, 155, 155n
Pierre, 133–136, 140, 189n
relation to Ishmael and Ahab, 44
see also *Moby-Dick*
Metaphor:
artificiality in, 182
cognitive function of, 174, 175, 177, 185

versus conceptual thought, 168n
contradiction in metaphorical process, 174
dead metaphor, 179
disparity in, 118, 164, 179
expectations in, 177, 185, 188
filtering action of, 165, 165n
fusion in, 164, 167
ineffable, 172n, 177, 177n
instability of, 182–184
integrity in, 184
myth, 180, 181
nature, 181
potentiality in, 177n
power of, 164
prayer, 170n
problem of, 174–177
provisional metaphor, 172, 176
reduction in, 117, 118, 165n, 177n
root metaphor, 165n
significance of versus logical significance, 169
simile and oxymoron, 184
stability in, 166
stages in life of, 167n, 179n
as structure, 165n, 173, 187
versus symbolic reduction, 170n
versus systematic thought, 183n
"third vocabulary" in, 168, 168n
"true" metaphor, 172n
unity in, 167, 170, 171
wilderness, 181
Moby-Dick, 12–46
compared to "Heart of Darkness," 62
compared to *Pierre*, 189n
compared to *The Confidence-Man*, 136
compared to *Ulysses*, 123
conception of language in, 28
as example of metaphorical instability, 184
Faulkner's assessment of, 154, 154n
figurative language, vague, in, 22
narrative techniques of, 12
narrative world of, 157
rhetoric of, 2
technique of allusion in, 17
technique of special languages in, 15

Moby-Dick (cont.)
  truth in, 40
  see also Ahab *and* Ishmael
Myth, 63, 64, 180

Narrative:
  as hunt, 4, 116, 158, 163*n*
  narrative form of *Absalom, Absalom!*, 101
  narrative structure as the individual consciousness, 125
  narrative technique and imaginative failure, 127
  narrative techniques of *Moby-Dick*, 12
  as search for narrative, 4, 116
  as simile, 103, 105
Narrator, emphasis on in modern fiction, 120
Nature, and metaphor, 181

O'Donnel, George M., 179, 180*n*
Oxymorons, 24, 184

Pepper, Stephen C., 165*n*
Poirier, Richard, 87*n*

Reality:
  in "Heart of Darkness," 55, 60
  for Marlow, 52, 58, 60
Rhetoric, of "Heart of Darkness," *Moby-Dick,* and *Absalom, Absalom!*, 2
Richards, I. A., 164

Shreve, 75*n*
Silence, 25, 98, 102
Simile:
  as failure to compose metaphor, 119

ineffable, 172
metaphor, 37, 184
as narrative method in *Absalom, Absalom!*, 105
Slatoff, Walter J., 149, 163*n*, 175*n*
Stream of consciousness, 121
Sutpen, Thomas:
  action toward Charles Bon, 87
  blackness, 89
  compared to Ahab, 82, 85, 95, 103
  compared to Quentin Compson, 100
  death of, 97
  design, 85–97
  history of, 81–96
  impotence of, 84, 87*n*
  innocence of, 83, 93
  metaphor, 116
  progress of, 91
  vision of, 89, 93, 95, 98, 128

Thematic conflicts in "Heart of Darkness," *Moby-Dick,* and *Absalom, Absalom!*, 10
Tristram Shandy, 155
Truth:
  in "The Bear," 161
  for Marlow, 52
  in *Moby-Dick,* 40
Turbayne, C. M., 164*n*, 167*n*, 172*n*, 179*n*, 186

Warren, Robert Penn, 135*n*
Wheelwright, Philip, 168*n*
Whiteness, 22–28, 82, 113
Wilderness, idea of, 181
Wimsatt, W. K., 163*n*
Woolf, Virginia, 121*n*, 125
Wuthering Heights, 155